T0215035

Model-Driven Software Systems Development Using the Meta-Artifact Process

The importance of architecture for software systems is widely accepted, but the role of architecture in the overall development process is not so clear. Presenting an architecture-centric process, *Model-Driven Software Systems Development Using the Meta-Artifact Process* makes the role of architecture clear. At its core, this book is about developing software systems and, more specifically, software code. It describes three major innovations for making software, which are combined with five widely used enabling technologies, to provide a complete, hypothesis-driven software development process known as Meta-Artifact Process (MAP). Having complete requirements is essential for making good software and supports the hypothesis-driven MAP.

MAP offers properties, qualities, and capabilities that help stakeholders and developers understand and reason about a domain and target systems of interest. MAP, through the central role of the Meta-Artifact and incorporating the view that a computer program is a hypothesis about the requirements, offers new ways to look at systems and their development, even changing the roles of developers and stakeholders.

Recommending agile methods wherever appropriate while supporting the OMG Essence standard and working within an overarching architecture, MAP presents ways to ensure that the requirements are complete and correct. It helps to identify likely points during development to form alternative hypotheses about them. Because MAP requires an underlying software development process, it can provide that clarity to existing processes in which the organization's developers are already proficient.

This book provides concrete examples from two broad but diverse areas—Accounting Information Systems in the commercial area and a military command and control system—to show the wide applicability of MAP in both commercial and defense domains.

Model-Driven Software Systems Development Using the Meta-Artifact Process

Wayne O'Brien

CRC Press
Taylor & Francis Group
Boca Raton London New York

CRC Press is an imprint of the
Taylor & Francis Group, an **informa** business
AN AUERBACH BOOK

First edition published 2024
2385 NW Executive Center Drive, Suite 320, Boca Raton FL 33431

and by CRC Press
4 Park Square, Milton Park, Abingdon, Oxon, OX14 4RN

CRC Press is an imprint of Taylor & Francis Group, LLC

© 2024 Taylor & Francis Group, LLC

ISBN: 978-1-032-58121-7 (hbk)
ISBN: 978-1-032-58176-7 (pbk)
ISBN: 978-1-003-44889-1 (ebk)

DOI: 10.1201/9781003448891

Typeset in Garamond
by Newgen Publishing UK

To my wife and three sons for their important encouragement over the years as I completed this book. My wife provided editorial suggestions and showed me patience and support throughout what became a long project.

Contents

Preface

Views of computer programming have changed over the years. My experience started with machine language programming for various machines, followed by assembly languages, and higher-level languages. Throughout, my colleagues and I drew pictures to figure out what was going on. I enthusiastically switched to the Unified Modeling Language (UML) and Model-Driven Development (MDD) when they were available. This eliminated the separate step of drawing a picture to see what was going on, because the visual model was not only the picture, but the picture actually determined what was going on. Yet in tutoring college students currently taking introductory Computer Science courses, I found that using Commercial off-the-shelf (COTS) software applications such as word processors, spreadsheets, and databases with their powerful capabilities and integration was considered programming. This was anticipated and approved of years ago by Mordecai Ben-Ari [5].

Nevertheless, traditional programming at the coding level remains at the center of computer science:

> Computer programming is at the heart of computer science. It is the implementation portion of software development, application development and software engineering efforts, transforming ideas and theories into actual, working solutions [26].

Still, not everyone likes to code. When I tutor middle schoolers, I like to tell them (they would say I share it with them) that word problems (which they either hate or consider the hardest of all the exercises) are like programming, where the words are the requirements and the mathematical expressions are the program statements. Sadly, this only convinces most of them that they don't want to become programmers. They might, however, think MDD was more attractive. MDD would not only allow them to see what was going on in their programs by producing and allowing access to the code, it would fit better in their comfort zone of visual interaction with games, COTS, and smartphone apps, as well as being less tedious. MDD allows both low-level programming and visual manipulation (e.g., for hypothesizing as discussed next).

As with mathematics, computer programming is analytical, logical, and at times, creative. Viewed as a hypothesis, a computer program is also scientific. It predicts that certain results will be produced and certain qualities that are consistent with the requirements will be exhibited when tested with specified data. In this sense, the requirements are the reality on which the program (hypothesis) is based.[1] This aspect of requirements emphasizes that getting the requirements right is crucial. As Einstein explained in his theory of relativity, reality in some circumstances is far different than reality in other circumstances. This book incorporates multiple ways to find requirements in difficult circumstances. It spends much time on ways to ensure that the reality is complete and correct and identifies likely points during development to form alternative hypotheses (throughout the text, as well as the Step Summary and the Diagram of Steps), which may range from algorithms, to architecture, to displays and documents.

When the computer program (in the form of MDD executables) produces consistently positive results upon sufficient testing, it is placed in production, analogously to the acceptance of a scientific theory [25]. Eventually, the program may fail when some untested processing possibility occurs, causing modifications (in a way that is visible to all stakeholders, using *this book*) until the program again runs according to specifications or is simply removed from production or deprecated in favor of a different approach to meeting the need. This is equivalent to a scientist's observing some phenomenon that an accepted theory does not explain, resulting in modification or rejection of the theory, based on further observation of the natural occurrence.

Note

1 Requirements can also be viewed as the reality about which observations can be made. These observations are either explicit specifications or implied by explicit specifications. As with the word problems mentioned earlier, there usually are many words in requirements that actually say nothing of what the system must do. The analogy breaks down a little in that the impact of the test data (event) is not on the requirements (reality) but on the hypothesis. That is, a hypothesis about a natural occurrence predicts that specified observations (results) will be made when specified natural or constructed events are encountered by the natural occurrence. For a program, the prediction is that when the program processes (encounters) specified data, it will produce specified results (observations), but the reality (the requirements) is not involved. Another difference is that the requirements are an artifact rather than a natural occurrence. However, this is not unique. For example, economies described by economics are artifacts, vast as they may be. As with requirements for software, economies themselves may be immaterial, but they reflect material reality. Nevertheless, economies may encounter events and responses may be compared to hypothetical predictions made

by an economic theory. The economic hypotheses or theories themselves do not produce the actual responses. Programs, on the other hand, produce the actual responses. Unlike an economy or a natural occurrence, it is possible to know precisely why and how a program responds as it does to specified data.

About the Author

Wayne O'Brien received his PhD in information technology and engineering in 2006 from George Mason University and became a certified architect in 2009, architecting systems as an engineering fellow for one of the major defense contractors. His doctoral dissertation, "Breakdowns in Controls in Automated Systems," was published in book form in the United States and Europe in December of 2008.

Chapter 1

Introduction

Model-Driven Software Systems Development Using the Meta-Artifact Process, a *guide for making software* (*MSW*) can be used for large or small systems[1], using agile methods [42,59] wherever appropriate, while supporting the OMG Essence standard, and working within an overarching architecture. *MSW* is concerned in particular with software systems, specifically software codes. Unless specified otherwise, the words *system* or *software* or *program*[2] or *code* refer to this software code. In some references to hypotheses, program is used as including all aspects of a software system, such as its architecture.

MSW works in conjunction with an organization's existing processes, especially Model-Driven Development (MDD). Some familiarity with MDD is useful but not essential to understand the ideas. However, if you are already an MDD practitioner, you can begin applying the Meta-Artifact Process (MAP), which underlies *MSW,* immediately (see Chapter 7). As a middle ground, some of the subheadings are appended with "Detailed Discussion" and may be safely skipped if you are otherwise an experienced practitioner and you want a shortcut to applying the procedure.

This ability to jump right in is one of the purposes of this guide. It allows the practitioner who is already using MDD to one extent or another to apply MAP quickly, because MAP builds on MDD. Programmers who do not have MDD experience, including some of its constituent technologies, could use one of various training methods to get sufficiently proficient, such as the excellent tutorials built into MDD tools.

MDD is inherently supportive of methods that continuously integrate development and deployment, while ensuring compliance with security requirements and the architecture. MAP encourages such methods by incorporating support for the idea that a program is a hypothesis (see Preface) about the requirements—the code does not need to be viewed as a rigid solution. Viewing the program as only a hypothesis, developers can use MDD to quickly test the current hypothesis and should not hesitate to revise it based on the results. The revised hypothesis is not limited to minor code changes but might include alternative algorithms, design changes to the human–computer interface, and changes to the architecture. All such changes would need to follow the organization's established review and approval procedures, such as compliance with the approved enterprise architecture and buy-in from the relevant stakeholders.

MAP with its enabling extensions, and the infrastructure of the enabling technologies on which MAP depends, provides a complete procedure (see Chapter 7) for making software-intensive systems. MAP addresses significant needs of highly integrated software-intensive systems in network-centric environments. For a working example of the application of the complete MAP, see Prototype in [58].

The Meta-Artifact offers properties, qualities, and capabilities that help stakeholders and developers understand and reason about a domain and target systems of interest. MAP, through the central role of the Meta-Artifact, and incorporating the view that a computer program is a hypothesis about the requirements, offers new ways to look at systems and their development, even changing the roles of developers and stakeholders, as discussed in Chapter 8 (see [58] for a detailed discussion).

There is extensive material in [58] related to demonstrating the superiority of the underlying process of *MSW* (Chapter 2) compared to other established processes, using properties, qualities, and capabilities (see the Properties, Qualities, and Capabilities—Detailed Discussion section) as metrics.[3] Figure 3.5 (Chapter 3) presents a comparison of MAP to an aggregate of well-established frameworks and concepts for current practice (e.g., Structured Analysis, OODA, Agile, Zachman, DoDAF/ UPDM, MDA), focusing on gaps among disciplines and phases. These gaps, which MAP eliminates or reduces, are a major cause of added costs and breakdowns in software systems.

There are also extensive references in [58], including many that are not usually thought of in conjunction with software. Further, [58] describes various technologies and concepts (e.g., object-oriented technology) in considerable detail, beyond what I considered appropriate for a guide.

MSW provides concrete examples from two broad but diverse areas of concern—Accounting Information Systems in the commercial area and C4ISR[4] in the military area—to show the wide applicability of MAP in both commercial and military domains. At an abstract level, the two areas have many overlaps. For example, military rules of engagement represent the same kind of volatile variability as business rules do in commercial systems (see Tables 4.4, 5.1, and 5.2). Military command and control follows the same logical flow as the traditional management process found in the major schools of management thought (see Glossary, Figure G.3, and [28]). More generally, the control model for the management process relates to the first-order feedback (closed-loop) system of cybernetics or systems theory [32].

A comprehensive, executable prototype that demonstrates all of the properties, qualities, and capabilities of MAP is included in [58].

Approach

MDD enables involvement of nontechnical stakeholders in using the Meta-Artifact recursively, which in turn ensures use of the agreed upon architecture (see the Recursive Use of Meta-Artifact and Special-Purpose Views sections and Chapter 6). Such involvement also ensures thorough elicitation of requirements (what the system should and should not do [9]), including nonfunctional or quality requirements (e.g., ease of use, reliability, and cybersecurity). Starting with a picture of what the program would do in MDD, rather than with the code for how the program would do it, offers the opportunity to hypothesize (as discussed in the preface) by visual manipulation before the program is cast in concrete. This hypothesizing could be done by some or all stakeholders, using special-purpose views (see Glossary) tailored to a stakeholder or a group of stakeholders (see the Special-Purpose Views section).

There are multiple steps where it would be especially appropriate for stakeholders to engage in such hypothesizing (see Step Summary). Depending on the results of the hypothesizing, certain steps would need to be repeated. When the stakeholders have made their changes to the model, they could then generate executables for the components they changed to validate their new hypothesis for the system.

The architecture would be an important part of the solution to the stakeholders because of their close involvement, rather than a somewhat arcane technical feature. As stakeholders, this would also be true of developer disciplines who otherwise tend to view the architecture as a technical nicety or even obstacle. Agreeing on an architecture at the beginning and adhering to it throughout the life of the system has multiple benefits (see Chapter 6), such as built-in cybersecurity across the life of the system. Other key byproducts of *MSW* are highlighted in the next section.

Goals

MSW emphasizes reducing total lifecycle costs. The goal is to make[5] systems that are correct, complete, architecturally consistent (see Chapter 6), and easy to maintain through recursive use of the Meta-Artifact. Meta-Artifact Process takes its name from the interactive Meta-Artifact, the result of integrating all of the artifacts of a system, for its entire life, using integrated modeling tools (see Glossary) for MDD (used in *MSW* because it is more precise than the sometimes used, often marketing-oriented term Visual Software Development or VSD).

Efficient code is largely dealt with through auto-code generation, linked to visible artifacts; justification for further improvements would be a cost–benefit decision. Any desired or required documentation is produced from the Meta-Artifact as a byproduct by MAP (see Figure 3.4), with no costly overhead activity or interference with agile methods. Documentation prepared in this way from the Meta-Artifact is always 100 percent current and accurate.

As with documentation, continuous integration and delivery or deployment are byproducts of MAP, based on the code auto-generated at the end of each iteration and the ongoing collaboration of stakeholders during development and operations. Code, subject to frequent change, such as business rules (see section Business Rules and Volatile Variability—Detailed Discussion), has a major impact on maintenance costs. *MSW* reduces these costs through the Bifurcated Architecture (see Chapter 5). Because of its emphasis on stakeholder involvement and MDD, *MSW* often requires only low code for programmers and no code for stakeholders. Its novel approach to MDD using the Meta-Artifact in MAP keeps *MSW* compatible with the OMG Essence standard for engineering methods.[6]

Role of Requirements

The starting point for processes used to make systems is determining the requirements for the system to be made, including nonfunctional or quality requirements. The first requirement to be considered is why the system is needed and what it needs to do (its purpose). As noted in the preface, requirements serve as the reality for the software, and the software's purpose is the core of its requirements. The system's purpose or the reasons the system is needed and the things it needs to do serve as guides for all other requirements. Requirements are not all apparent, because they involve both explicit knowledge and tacit knowledge (see Glossary). *MSW* emphasizes the role of requirements and offers new ways of finding and turning them into systems that are robust during their entire lifetime.

The basis for software projects may be totally new requirements with no existing system, or some mix of new requirements and existing code. There may be more than meets the eye for requirements, but they are the ingredients of good software, as they represent the reality that the software fulfills. The part that doesn't meet the eye may result in a broken system, so *MSW* spends considerable time discussing how to see what may be unseen. *MSW* dwells a little on how to elicit and represent requirements (as artifacts in the Meta-Artifact). If this is unnecessary for you, you may want to go directly to Chapter 7 (also presented as an activity diagram in Figure 7.3; for extensive detail on the steps, see [58]). In addition to volatile variability, missed, ignored, or poorly understood requirements (technical debt[7]), including quality attributes, are major causes of high maintenance costs. Beyond technical debt, evolving and new requirements have a major impact on lifecycle costs. *MSW* reduces technical debt by emphasizing ways to fully elicit requirements, including tacit knowledge (see the Knowledge Management Overview section) and domain rules (see the

Domain Rules—Detailed Discussion section), then auto-generating the necessary code; it reduces the cost of evolving and new requirements through *MSW*'s three extensions and five enablers (see Table 4.1**)**.

When a program fails to produce correct results, the fault may lie in an incorrect interpretation of the requirements or missing requirements. Missing requirements may be tacit or due to drift from the original problem. Before adding requirements (creep) the original problem should be reviewed. New requirements (even newly revealed tacit or missing requirements) should be added only if they are within the original problem scope. Otherwise, approval to expand the scope should be sought to avoid requirements creep. Changes to a program, for whatever reason, are the cause of much additional testing and the source of many future problems [44]. New requirements are a common cause of such changes. Examining why such changes arise and reducing the additional testing and the problems are major concerns of MSW, both for planned and unplanned changes.

Explicit and Tacit Knowledge

Explicit knowledge may be active (embedded in human consciousness [57] or passive (see Glossary)). Tacit knowledge is implicit knowledge that is experience-related, applied unconsciously, or taken for granted [61,65]. Such implicit knowledge must be captured—that is, identified, extracted, and stored as artifacts (see Figure 2.1 for examples) for use in making the system.

In addition to explicit knowledge about requirements, tacit knowledge of requirements may be involved in two ways. First, people may perform activities as routines that they give little or no thought to, especially the reasons for performing them. The following story illustrates this. Whenever a certain cook prepared a roast, he cut it in half and placed it in two pans. After observing this a number of times, one of his assistants asked him why. He said his grandmother had always done it that way. When the cook's grandmother paid him a visit, the assistant took the opportunity to ask her why she cooked roasts that way. She said that the pans she had were too small to hold the entire roast. If a new automated system were based on the cook's tacit knowledge (in this case, performing a routine based on the implicit assumption that there was good reason to do so in a certain way), an unnecessary step—always cutting the roast in half—would be included.

Second, an automated system to be replaced by a new system may perform functions that are not known or incompletely known to the people using the system, perhaps because the automated system to be replaced is undocumented. If such unknown or incompletely known functions are not performed by the new system, their absence may go undetected until the effect becomes visible in the results produced by the new system, e.g., an erroneous calculation or a certain type of error that had been detected by a missing function. I have worked with government systems—used in the management of multi-billion-dollar programs—that had 30-year-old embedded algorithms that were undocumented and whose use maintenance programmers could not determine. To err on the side of not having undetected problems, the algorithms were routinely carried over to new systems. In another case, the daily process for reconciling a number of multi-billion-dollar financial systems with each other never fell within the requirements of any of the systems, so the reconciliation was approximated manually, sometimes days after the fact. Eventually, the task was automated by the people responsible for the manual reconciliation, using their budget and without formal requirements. The automated process ran daily and reconciled the systems to the proverbial penny.

As the examples show, the consequence of tacit knowledge may be either to include something that is not needed or to risk omitting something that is. Likewise, failure to capture all relevant explicit and tacit knowledge in the requirements for an automated system may result in inclusion of unnecessary features or omission of necessary ones, because the program is based on a misconception of reality. Stated in another way, some requirements may be either missing or unnecessary, whether because of tacit knowledge or failure to capture relevant explicit knowledge. Perhaps the most common causes of not capturing all relevant knowledge of the system are not identifying all relevant sources (e.g., not talking to the grandmother) and not extracting such knowledge (e.g., not asking the grandmother the right question). These factors contribute to causing requirements defects (contributing to technical debt), one of the larger categories of software error [44].

Knowledge Management Overview

MSW applies knowledge management theory [61] to the issues of tacit versus explicit knowledge, including the organizational and cultural (tacit) knowledge that is related to the transformation from manual processes and automated systems being replaced (that may have tacit knowledge embedded in them). To accomplish this, Knowledge Management uses three constructs or lenses to look at knowledge: breakdowns (the term includes the traditional sense of a system breakdown), narratives, and time (see Glossary). Knowledge management theory is useful in converting tacit knowledge into explicit knowledge for requirements. Knowledge management is also useful in avoiding gaps (see the Gaps section), related to tacit knowledge.

MSW focuses on requirements as the starting point for the system to be made. This focus encourages the capture of all relevant requirements through knowledge management and Domain Rules, in addition to the usual techniques—avoiding both the inclusion of unnecessary features and the omission of necessary ones.

Failing to meet requirements is viewed both in the context of experience and the theoretical context of knowledge management. In knowledge management terms, requirements exist as both explicit and tacit knowledge [22,57,61,63,64,65]. Requirements for all stakeholders (see Glossary) must be extracted from both explicit and tacit knowledge to reduce the number of missing requirements (incompleteness) as well as the number of unnecessary requirements. One of the new concepts introduced in *MSW*, Domain Rules, offers a means to reduce both by bounding the problem domain.

Tacit knowledge of requirements is a challenge for elicitation of requirements. Whether embedded in tacit knowledge or more readily available as explicit knowledge or information (see Glossary), MAP makes requirements quickly accessible to all authorized stakeholders throughout the lifecycle of the system. Along with the causes described in this section, tacit requirements result from evolving technology, breakdowns, and gaps. In addition to its role in tacit requirements, evolving technology can drive the need for new or modified requirements over the life of the system. The impact of evolving technology, breakdowns, and gaps is described in detail in Chapter 2.

Notes

1 A set or arrangement of elements that are organized to accomplish some predefined goal by processing information [67]. *MSW* focuses on systems of software programs.

2 An element of a system consisting of software code.

3 These metrics should be helpful if you want to evaluate *MSW* against other methodologies.

4 Command, Control, Communications, Computers, Intelligence, Surveillance, and Reconnaissance.

5 In keeping with the name of this guide, I have generally substituted some form of "make" for corresponding forms of "develop," but generally left alone the familiar phrases such as "systems development" or "developer discipline."

6 MAP, as its name suggests, is a high-level process, yet is used to generate the lowest level of a software system, its code. MAP can easily accommodate the Kernel Alphas and Activity Spaces, either explicitly (e.g., by assigning alphas and activity spaces to steps in the procedure (Step Summary)) or as byproducts using special purpose views (Special-Purpose Views).

7 Missed or poorly understood requirements are included in technical debt along with ignored (or postponed) requirements because they may be generally avoided by thoroughly eliciting and analyzing requirements through a proper focus on the problem space (e.g., see Chapter 4).

Chapter 2

Meta-Artifact Process

MAP, the basis for *MSW*, is a process for making software-intensive systems that adds three extensions to five existing enabling technologies (see Table 4.1; [15,29,56,67,75]).

MAP is an instance of MDD, an approach for making software-intensive systems, based on visual representations of artifacts [38]. It combines the UML with automatic code generating tools (Glossary, integrated modeling tools).

As an instance of MDD, MAP uses MDD to produce and manage the Meta-Artifact, which contains the artifacts for an entire domain, including patterns and components from which software-intensive systems can be composed. The core UML model of MAP is also compatible with Model Driven Architecture (MDA).[1]

Dynamic Interdependence of the Eight Elements of MAP

Figure 2.1, representing the overall flow of the MAP, shows the dynamic interdependence of the eight elements of MAP—the three extensions (labeled Ex1–Ex3) and five enablers (labeled

DOI: 10.1201/9781003448891-2

MAP – 3 Extensions and 5 Enablers

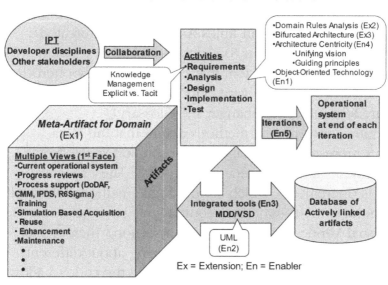

Figure 2.1   Dynamic Interdependence of the Eight Elements of MAP—First Face of Meta-Artifact.

En1–En5) of Table 4.1. MAP uses knowledge management to discover system requirements that may be hidden as tacit knowledge as well as explicit requirements. In terms of Figure 2.1, knowledge management techniques would be applied, as shown, during the requirements and analysis activities of each iteration, in order to convert previously tacit knowledge into active knowledge for transformation into passive knowledge (see Glossary) in the form of artifacts in the Meta-Artifact. With the iterative, incremental development methods referenced in Table 4.1, each iteration includes the full set of development activities (core workflows in [9]).

The interdependence of the eight elements is central to ensuring that MAP maintains adherence to the domain-wide architecture (architecture centricity), which tends to deteriorate entropically (see Chapter 3). Domain Rules Analysis (see Chapter 4) uses domain rules to characterize and establish the boundaries of the domain and to increase the completeness of the Meta-Artifact in representing the entire domain. In conjunction with Domain Rules Analysis, the Bifurcated Architecture (see Chapter 5) separates volatile variability (those aspects of the system that change relatively often) from commonality and stable variability (those aspects of the system that are less subject to change; see Glossary).

Iterative, incremental methods assure that the Meta-Artifact represents the totality of the solution space, from requirements through executable artifacts. The executable artifacts (increments, which support agile methods) allow all stakeholders to see whether requirements have been met (see the Visual Verification and Validation section). Incremental development also facilitates hypothesizing about different approaches by having the model generate the code to allow all stakeholders to examine actual results of the different approaches, without the time and effort to write code manually and create resistance to discarding it. During the early increments, even the architecture may not be settled. When stakeholders see the system in operation, they may hypothesize that structural or other architectural changes would improve the system's effectiveness (e.g., intuitive sequence) or efficiency (e.g., performing similar functions in the same place with the same reference file).

Object-Oriented Technology (OOT) provides by its nature certain capabilities that enhance adherence to the architecture— inheritance for reuse and reliability, encapsulation for security and interoperability, and polymorphism for abstraction and extensibility. The UML provides a formal graphical notation for OOT, which results in a common representation for all of the artifacts of systems development. Integrated modeling tools (Glossary) leverage this common representation to capture, manipulate, and manage the artifacts of development for a system, from the highest-level semantics of broadly stated functional and nonfunctional requirements through operating or executing components, comprising the Meta-Artifact. Together, the five enablers provide the technology infrastructure for producing and managing the Meta-Artifact, which is described in detail in Chapter 3.

Gaps

On the basis of historical evidence [3, 12, 13, 14, 15, 17, 19, 31, 51, 66, 67, 69, 74], it can be said that lifecycle-centric systems development in practice suffers from disconnects (gaps) among the phases[2] of software development and developer disciplines throughout the lifecycle, leading to increased costs, technical debt, and defects for the system. The impact of these gaps (see Figure 3.5 for a graphical representation of gaps) is compounded for systems that must interact with other systems. That is, the gaps among phases and disciplines in making a single system are increased by the completely different development cycles of separate systems.

Roles of Knowledge Management, and Selected Extensions and Enablers in Mitigating Gaps— Detailed Discussion

Knowledge Management

In knowledge management terms, the gaps result from missing narratives and/or the practical means of converting narratives into explicit knowledge, because of the form (artifacts) the narratives are in or the tools available. Breakdowns occur when developers for the next phase try to apply the knowledge and routines of their disciplines against a tacit background that differs from that of the preceding discipline (semantic gaps, see Figure 3.5). That is, the explicit knowledge as well as the tacit knowledge of the disciplines differs. Over time, the explicit knowledge from the previous phase (or another discipline) recedes to history (see Glossary, tacit knowledge and time) in the background of that phase, making it less accessible to the next phase with the passage of time (temporal gaps).

The lenses of time, breakdowns, and narratives can be applied to reverse the entropic dynamics of the semantic and temporal gaps. *MSW* focuses stakeholder attention on the need to recover the embedded knowledge by identifying gaps during each increment, before tacit knowledge recedes into the background. Developers can reconstruct the tacit knowledge through narratives that retrace the temporal sequence of actions (reverse the knowledge creating dynamics; see Glossary, narratives), still available during the increment, but not yet captured in the Meta-Artifact, e.g., decisions made during the previous increment. When delayed, this can become a costly, duplicative effort encountered in system maintenance activities performed on operational systems that lack current, comprehensive documentation. Due at least in part to such circumstances, system lifecycle maintenance accounts for the majority of lifecycle costs, including technical debt, [44]. Changes to software source code for maintenance are costly and have a high probability of introducing defects into the system [44] (see Chapter 5).

Extensions and Enablers

Making systems with the UML, iterative and incremental methods, and visual models for MDD linked to running systems, in addition to the benefits already noted, mitigates the gaps shown in Figure 3.5.

The UML mitigates semantic gaps through its common representation across disciplines, workflow activities, iterations, phases, and individual systems. Iterative and incremental methods mitigate both semantic and temporal gaps by performing the complete set of work flow activities (e.g., requirements, analysis, design, and implementation in the Unified Software Development Process (USDP)) within an iteration in a relatively short time, increasing the availability of current artifacts and encouraging close collaboration among all disciplines at all levels of detail (i.e., requirements through implementation). This completeness and close collaboration also support the opportunity to test alternative hypotheses for both the architecture and the program. The mitigation is weakened by the time that elapses between iterations and the even greater amount of time that may elapse between phases (groups of iterations in USDP) and systems; the availability of current artifacts and their developers, for reference or collaboration, decreases as the elapsed time increases.

Two additional considerations increase the likelihood of semantic gaps between systems. First, while a common representation may be used for all of the systems, they are likely to have different architectures with different semantics, to the extent that artifacts and those who created them for previous systems are not employed to produce subsequent systems. Second, the artifacts representing the different systems are likely to reside in different repositories, which interferes with access (see Chapter 3 regarding accessibility of artifacts) to the systems' artifacts. Both of these considerations hinder making subsequent systems in terms of reuse and interoperability, but are mitigated by the Meta-Artifact.

The creation of visual models for MDD that are linked to a running system, through automatic code generation or other means such as the transformation process in MDA [60], would increase the likelihood of retaining accessible artifacts that accurately represent the running system, reducing semantic gaps and the impact of temporal gaps on making that system. However, the focus on one system at a time continues to cause semantic gaps compounded by temporal gaps. The one-system focus would be mitigated by the Meta-Artifact and Domain Rules Analysis (see Chapters 3 and 4).

Further Benefits of MAP—Detailed Discussion

MAP, as summarized graphically in Figure 2.1, using the mitigation techniques described in the Extensions and Enablers section, guided by the Meta-Artifact (new versions of the Meta-Artifact are based on the previous one, see the Recursive Use of Meta-Artifact section), further reduces semantic and temporal gaps, especially those among systems, in the ways described next.

Capture Domain Knowledge

MAP ensures that knowledge about the systems in a domain is captured in the Meta-Artifact as passive knowledge in the form of artifacts (e.g., narratives and diagrams) that preserve the semantics of a system across iterations, phases, and systems (the Meta-Artifact contains artifacts for all systems in a domain, but subsequent references in this context will frequently use "system," rather than "system in a domain," for brevity). Stakeholders could form hypotheses using animated views of the artifacts based on the knowledge captured in any increment, once step 9 of the procedure had been reached for the increment (see Step Summary). Such early assessment would test the completeness of knowledge capture and allow consideration of alternate views at all levels, including the architecture. The knowledge management section in the next chapter contains additional details about preserving knowledge of the system.

Recursive Use of Meta-Artifact

MAP uses the Meta-Artifact recursively to guide the making of new artifacts, which automatically extend the Meta-Artifact as they are added to the repository (see Chapter 3 for discussion of placing artifacts in the repository); that is, MAP uses the Meta-Artifact to produce results that extend the Meta-Artifact. With the integrated modeling tools, MAP converts the information represented in artifacts of previous development into active knowledge on which to base the generation of new artifacts that are consistent with the baseline architecture captured in the Meta-Artifact (see the next bullet). This conversion is temporally independent, preventing the knowledge about previous development from becoming tacit with the passage of time (see Chapter 3 regarding knowledge entropy). The new artifacts may be derived through specialization, based on decomposition or other reuse, or related to previous artifacts only through the baseline architecture.

Domain-Wide Focus

MAP's domain-wide focus produces the Meta-Artifact with artifacts for an entire domain, including patterns and components from which target systems can be composed, before completing generation of any target systems. MAP uses these domain-wide artifacts to capture the baseline architecture for a domain in the Meta-Artifact, during the early iterations of development. All systems made from the Meta-Artifact for a domain incorporate the common baseline architecture; MAP applies domain-wide architecture centricity.

The early development of a domain-wide architecture and artifacts ensures that high-level semantic artifacts for new target systems, in addition to more detailed artifacts from any previous target systems, are available in the Meta-Artifact. Producing domain-wide artifacts during initial development avoids the impact of temporal gaps involving overall domain knowledge, especially from domain experts whose availability if subsequent systems were made would be problematic. Retaining these domain-wide artifacts in the Meta-Artifact in a single repository makes their transformation into active knowledge (see Glossary) through the integrated modeling tools temporally independent.

Single Repository

Using a single repository for all artifacts for a domain (see Chapter 3 for discussion of placing artifacts in the repository), managed by integrated modeling tools, avoids temporal gaps related to identifying and accessing needed artifacts during subsequent development for the domain.

Team Continuity

MAP also deals with the practical issues of keeping the same team members available during the time needed to make multiple systems by allowing them to stay productive without moving to an unrelated project. Traditional systems development processes focus on one system at a time, increasing the likelihood of the intersystem gaps noted in the Extensions and Enablers section.

Because of MAP's domain-wide focus, different disciplines can work in parallel on artifacts for a domain and for multiple systems. Domain experts can proceed with aspects of a domain that do not affect the first system, while developers begin work on the first system. When team members for a discipline finish their work on an iteration for the first system, they can move to the next system, then return to the first system, increasing the likelihood that at least a core team for each discipline could work on all phases of a system. Knowledge gained from the second system could be applied in making alternative hypotheses for programs in the first system. To the extent that such parallel activities can be sustained using at least the same core members for each discipline, the team members can continue increasing and applying their expertise, further reducing semantic gaps (see Figure 3.5). Organizations would need to consider changes in their approval and budgeting patterns, as well as their project management practices, to take full advantage of domain-wide parallelism.

Within an iteration, each functional discipline works through each activity with little or no specialization between activities, because of using the same notation to reduce or eliminate semantic gaps among disciplines (see fragmented views shown in Figure 3.5).

The developers do not hand off work to each other in serial manner. Instead, they work together throughout the effort, evolving levels of detail to address their areas of concern. One of the chief goals—and challenges—of an engineering process and an architecture framework is to provide a means for the various development stakeholders to communicate and align their design decisions [11].

The artifacts produced for each activity for each discipline are automatically placed in the database by the tools (see Figure 2.1). The tools can then access the artifacts in the database to produce views of the Meta-Artifact as needed, reconverting the information captured in the artifacts—including tacit knowledge—into active knowledge.

Impact of Evolving Technology on Requirements

Evolving technology can drive the need for new or modified requirements over the life of the system, due to the following considerations:

1. Opportunities and requirements for new systems
2. Needs for new and modified requirements for the current system, e.g., online support for new customer technology
3. Uninterrupted integrity of existing requirements by avoiding obsolescence, e.g., new cybersecurity capabilities
4. More timely and less costly responses to new and modified requirements, e.g., support for no-code modifications directly by stakeholders responsible for the change
5. Revealing new requirements in systems and rendering current requirements obsolete, e.g., new federal regulations.

There are obstacles to satisfying the above considerations for changing existing systems, including the following:

1. Technology has led to systems that are (see Figures 2.2 and 2.3):
   1.1. Software intensive
   1.2. Highly integrated
   1.3. Network centric
2. The systems originally replaced human routines, established over long periods of time, that relied on:
   2.1. Physical records and barriers
   2.2. Time intervals for feedback sufficient for humans to react
   2.3. Interpersonal relationships
3. Explicit and tacit knowledge of needs may not be articulated as artifacts for the development, operation, and maintenance of the existing systems
4. The requirements background has receded farther to history

In any case, the content of the requirements, especially of Business Rules, is not simply declarative, but rather imperative and must therefore be assessed immediately. This review of an existing system is an especially good time to hypothesize about the system, including its architecture. Any aspect of the current system under review may be obsolete, including the architecture. Using *MSW*, the existing architecture should be reviewed for domain rules (see Domain Rules— Detailed Discussion) and bifurcation (see the Objective of Bifurcated Architecture—Detailed Discussion section), greater online support, and no-code or low-code capabilities for developers and other stakeholders. The visual model permits all stakeholders to observe the current architecture (e.g., its use cases and their relationships), try out changes, and form alternative hypotheses to represent the problem space. If a hypothesis appears to be worth pursuing, portions of the solution space can be generated from the alternative problem space for in-depth analysis to test the new, visually based hypothesis.

Hidden Risks of Increasing Automation—Detailed Discussion

Requirements are particularly sensitive to the confrontation between long-standing human procedures and evolving technology. Current computerized systems contain tacit knowledge of requirements for manual systems that they replaced, perhaps over multiple upgrades. The manual systems in areas such as accounting evolved over centuries, relying on personal interaction, creating many layers of Tacit Knowledge within the requirements background as Explicit Knowledge receded to history with each upgrade (see Glossary). Decades of automation have steadily attempted to complement, substitute for, or obviate manual procedures.

The overall risk born by an enterprise's computerized systems increases as the reliance on them expands. Risk is defined as the product of the likelihood of a breakdown and the impact of the breakdown. The breakdown may be caused by a missing requirement or weakness in the implementation.

Figures 2.2 and 2.3 show graphically the impact on risk of the three technological factors as evolving technology replaces human routines and systems move into the northeast quadrants of those figures. As the proportion of an enterprise's activities that are automated increases, manual authorization and decision processes are replaced and the need for automation increases, causing the risk attributable to such need to increase. As the integration of these automated activities increases, the use of manual procedures decreases even more, causing the risk attributable to needed automation to increase further.

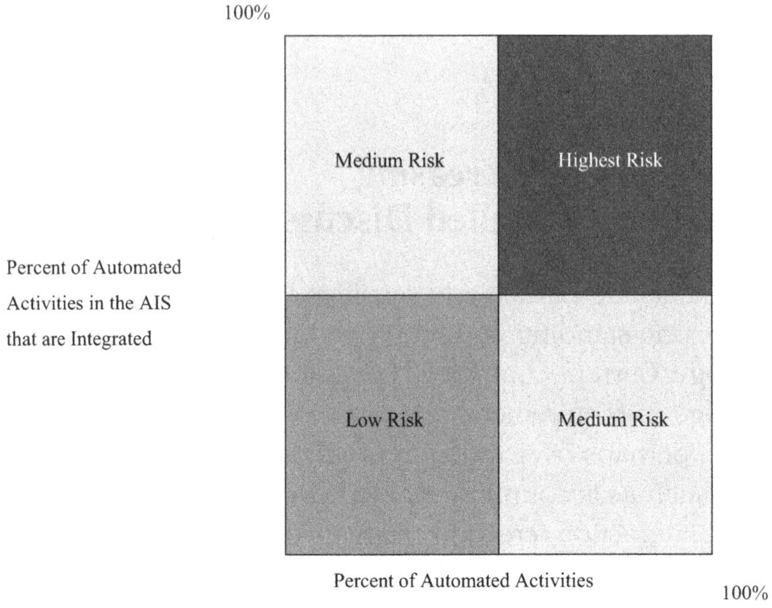

100%
Medium Risk
Highest Risk
Percent of Automated
Activities in the AIS
that are Integrated
Low Risk
Medium Risk
Percent of Automated Activities
100%

Figure 2.2 Integration of Automated Activities.

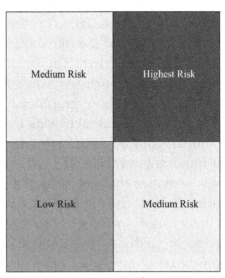

100%
Medium Risk
Highest Risk
Percent of Automated
Activities in the AIS
Dependent on Network-
Centric Applications
Low Risk
Medium Risk
Percent of Automated Activities
100%

Figure 2.3 Use of Network-Centric Applications.

Similarly, as automation increases and the proportion of automated activities that depend on network-centric applications increases, additional manual authorization and decision processes are replaced, increasing the reliance on automated procedures and the risk still more. The risks stemming from increased reliance on electronic forms of authorization and identification are compounded by the speed and physical separation with which electronically transmitted transactions occur.

The continual replacement of manual procedures is an example of embedding knowledge in systems. Unless the knowledge (both tacit and explicit) of needs and requirements is articulated as artifacts, the knowledge recedes to history (or farther to history, in the case of tacit knowledge) with the passage of time, making it extremely difficult to recover for any purpose, e.g., correcting breakdowns (see the Hidden Risks of Breakdowns—Detailed Discussion section), training, or operations.

The risks described in conjunction with Figures 2.2 and 2.3 arise from the deviation from the preexisting human routines and procedures and the background on which requirements are based. The result is unmet tacit requirements or breakdowns.

Hidden Risks of Breakdowns—Detailed Discussion

The hidden risks of increasing automation may cause breakdowns (see Glossary) as the likelihood of missed requirements increases through increased automation. Dealing with the technological factors (caused by the availability of and need for automation) may be compounded by a potential non-technological effect; there could be a routinization effect as people who interact with the system become increasingly familiar with its breakdowns and routinely compensate for them (see the example of manually reconciling large-scale systems in Chapter 1). Whenever improvements are considered, these tacit requirements should be targeted. Even in apparently smooth running and well-documented systems, tacit requirements may be lurking just out of sight. In fact, they may be covering up an opportunity for a new or modified system.

Initially, the concern is to build a new system that fulfills the requirements that have been accepted by the stakeholders. During the lifecycle of the system, the concern shifts to responding quickly and economically to new and changed requirements, while maintaining the integrity of the existing system. When such requirements are not responded to quickly enough, breakdowns occur, disrupting the routine functioning of the system. The impact of new requirements may be compounded by the impact of infusing new technology. New technology exposes new requirements, in addition to those exposed by new business or mission requirements.

Maintaining the integrity of the existing systems includes adhering to the established architecture. Changes in the architecture that appear to be necessary should be tested as a new hypothesis for meeting the new requirements (the new reality for the hypothesis).

Notes

1 MDA uses standards (including UML) developed by the Object Management Group [60]. It relies on a platform-independent model (PIM) in, e.g., UML and independent transforms to produce a platform-specific model (PSM). The PSM, with further transforms, is used to generate executable code for a selected platform. MAP tools (Glossary, Integrated Modeling Tools) have built-in transforms to generate executable code for a specified platform from a UML model.

2 The number and names of development phases differ among processes, but for brevity, *MSW* refers to the phases *requirements, analysis, design,* and *implementation,* which are also the names of the first four core workflows (development activities) within an iteration in the Unified Software Development Process (USDP [9]), which is the underlying process used by the procedure (see Procedure) for applying MAP.

Chapter 3

Meta-Artifact

The Meta-Artifact is the electronically linked set of all of the artifacts of development for all applications (systems) for a domain (see Figure 2.2). The linking is through hot links directly on the artifacts or a browser in the integrated modeling tools. Examples of artifacts are natural language narratives, graphical representations, or software code in various forms describing the desired and/or current systems. The electronic linking of all of the artifacts of development contributes to the Meta-Artifact's representation of the total solution space. The Meta-Artifact is amplified by the enabling technologies and extensions (see Table 4.1 and Figure 2.1) and the Meta-Artifact's recursive use in MAP for its own development (see recursive property in the Properties, Qualities, and Capabilities—Detailed Discussion section).

Properties, Qualities, and Capabilities—Detailed Discussion

The Meta-Artifact has six properties, five qualities, and five capabilities that define and describe it externally (see Tables 3.1, 3.2, 3.3). Figures 2.1, 3.1, 3.2, and 3.4 describe internal aspects

 DOI: 10.1201/9781003448891-3

Table 3.1   Meta-Artifact Properties

Property	Provision of Property
Current (Figure 2.1)	The artifacts are part of the Meta-Artifact stored in a model element database that is created and maintained by integrated modeling tools. The executing code for the demonstration is generated from the Meta-Artifact (see Prototype in [58])
Dynamic (Figure 2.1)	The Meta-Artifact contains the running system and provides views of the actual system, including all of its artifacts. The integrated tools allow multiple, animated views of the system, not just prescribed static views.
Prescriptive (Figure 2.1)	The Meta-Artifact generates the prescriptive code for the executing prototype.
Unifying (Figure 2.1)	The executable components of the prototype in [58] have a common user interface, shared databases, and direct interaction with each other. The use of integrated modeling tools based on the UML to recursively apply the Meta-Artifact ensures that artifacts of the Meta-Artifact have a common representation, a common architecture, and are accessible to all stakeholders.
Seen from multiple views with a common representation (Figure 2.1)	The Meta-Artifact is represented in the UML. The UML assures a common representation, with multiple views provided by the integrated tools.
Recursive (Figure 2.1)	The Meta-Artifact is applied recursively by the integrated modeling tools as new artifacts are generated from higher levels or their preceding versions. The result is a running system with a single architecture, providing a common framework and patterns for the generated executable components.

Table 3.2   Meta-Artifact Qualities

Quality	Provision of Quality
Stakeholder access to current views appropriate to their interest (Figure 3.4)	This quality is provided by the Current, Dynamic, and Multiple-View properties of the Meta-Artifact.
Animated, rather than static, views of development artifacts	The Dynamic and Multiple-View properties of the Meta-Artifact are activated by the integrated tools to provide this quality, e.g., animated views of the visual model.
Special-purpose views (Figure 3.4)	The Dynamic and Multiple-View properties of the Meta-Artifact are activated by the integrated tools to provide this quality, e.g., the 26 products defined by DoDAF.
Process and product are different views rather than separate things	All activities performed on the electronically linked artifacts of the Meta-Artifact lead directly to the objective system, through MAP's recursive use of the Meta-Artifact to automatically generate the system. The building of the Meta-Artifact in this recursive way provides a systematic process, without separate overhead activities, e.g., to prepare documentation and specifications.
Active semantic chain (Figures 2.1, G.1, and G.2)	All artifacts of the Meta-Artifact are electronically linked and accessible through the integrated modeling tools.

of the Meta-Artifact. The Results of Key Properties, Qualities, and Capabilities—Detailed Discussion section deals with their use in applying the Meta-Artifact.

All properties, qualities, and capabilities of the Meta-Artifact were demonstrated by the executable prototype. Adding

Table 3.3 Meta-Artifact Capabilities

Capability	Provision of Capability
1. Comprehensively articulate stakeholders' explicit and tacit knowledge of a domain as artifacts and a means to store the artifacts as information that can be converted back to explicit knowledge, to assure adequate understanding and proper implementation of requirements for the domain during the complete lifecycle of systems in the domain (Figure 2.1).	MAP begins with domain rules to cover the domain, and use cases to capture the domain rules. These artifacts capture the high-level semantics of the domain to support the initial realization of use cases into analysis classes [9] and related artifacts and for subsequent enhancement and maintenance activities using the integrated modeling tools.
2. Convert the information representing the artifacts of the domain into explicit knowledge to assure adequate understanding and proper implementation of requirements for the domain during the complete lifecycle of systems in the domain (Figure 2.1).	The artifacts are captured electronically as the Meta-Artifact in the database of electronically linked artifacts maintained by the integrated modeling tools used to create the artifacts. The tacit and explicit knowledge captured for the domain is available through the active semantic chain, which stakeholders can use through the tools to obtain views that provide the explicit knowledge they need at any time during a system's life.

(*continued*)

Table 3.3 (Continued)

Capability	Provision of Capability
3. Use the explicit knowledge of capability 2 to take account of existing systems and potential future systems in the domain during the complete lifecycle of the system under development, because of both the explicit and tacit knowledge contained in other systems on which the system under development may depend, especially when they must interact with each other.	The interactions of all use cases for the domain are represented in the UML. By applying the domain rules when realizing the use cases, the realization and implementation of the use cases, using the integrated modeling tools, inherently take account of other applications in the domain.
4. Produce an architecture that reduces or eliminates the disconnects (gaps) among development disciplines and development phases (Figure 3.5).	Chapter 7 allows the same team (consisting of representatives of each discipline) to apply all work flows during each iteration avoiding handoffs from discipline to discipline and phase to phase (see Figure 3.5).
5. Reduce the need to change software source code for maintenance resulting from breakdowns or changing needs due to volatile variability, with resulting reductions in costs and defects (Figure 5.1).	The Bifurcated Architecture uses a COTS inference engine to manage the prescriptive rules for the business rules identified during analysis and design (see Figure 5.1). Prescriptive rules can be changed directly by end users by making changes to the rules that are read as data by an inference engine.

and changing rules in the prototype was straightforward and easily verified, validating the basic premise of the Bifurcated Architecture (see Prototype in [58]).

Visual Representation of the Meta-Artifact

The Meta-Artifact is shown as the cube (Ex1) in the lower left-hand corner of Figure 2.1. The properties of the Meta-Artifact depend on the dynamic interplay of the eight elements shown in Figure 2.1 and described in the Dynamic Interdependence of the Eight Elements of MAP section. Many of the Meta-Artifact's properties, qualities, and capabilities depend in particular on the integrated modeling tools as well as the extensions and other enablers, allowing the interdependence of its eight elements to be dynamic (see Figure 2.1). The displayed face of the cube in Figure 2.1 shows examples of the multiple views embodied in the Meta-Artifact (see the Architecture Centricity section).

Paralleling these multiple views of the architecture, the Meta-Artifact itself has multiple dimensions—the Multiple Views, the Artifacts in the Meta-Artifact, and the Meta-Artifact Over Time, as shown by the cubes in Figure 2.1, Figure 3.1, and Figure 3.2. That is, set M = the Meta-Artifact, set i = a view, j = an artifact, and t = time. Then $M(i, j, t)$ would be view i of artifact j at time t.

As can be seen from the examples in the three diagrams, the artifacts of development are not limited to UML primitives, such as an object or association. They are more likely to be complex artifacts consisting of many such primitives. Nor are the artifacts of the Meta-Artifact limited to object-oriented representations or UML notation. Natural language documents such as solicitations (RFPs) and less formal requests are included. Because the artifacts include the software code, the running systems of the domain are also part of the Meta-Artifact.

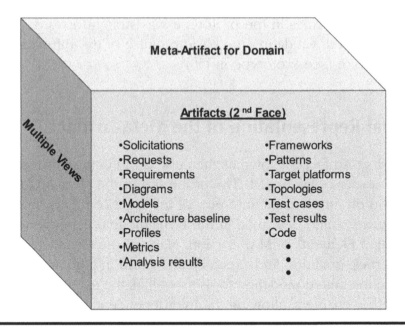

Figure 3.1   Artifacts in the Meta-Artifact—Second Face.

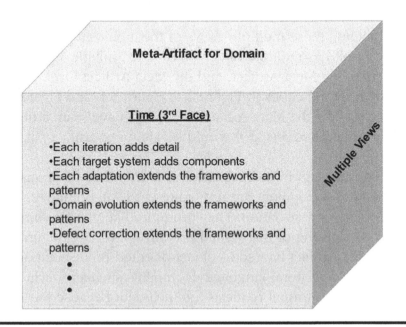

Figure 3.2   Meta-Artifact Over Time.

Knowledge Management Impact—Detailed Discussion

The Meta-Artifact provides a knowledge management narrative for all systems in the domain that makes the background (tacit knowledge represented by a system) explicit. Narratives in knowledge management serve as a basic organizing principle of human cognition.

> Narratives, articulated as texts, can be seen as material traces of learning and collective remembering processes, social imprints of a meaningful course of events, documents and records of human action. They allow people to articulate knowledge through discourse [61].

Through their electronic linking in the Meta-Artifact, all artifacts, including code, are part of the knowledge management narrative of the system and the domain. That is, through the recursive application of the Meta-Artifact in MAP and the active semantic chain, knowledge captured in the Meta-Artifact is purposefully converted into action and action into additional knowledge in the Meta-Artifact. The Meta-Artifact provides the structure and explicit representation of the knowledge about the system, when used in MAP, to prevent the entropy—loss of explicitness and structure—that would otherwise occur, by converting the tacit and explicit knowledge about the system into artifacts. The Meta-Artifact thus preserves the tacit and explicit knowledge of the system as information (in the form of artifacts) that can be converted into active knowledge, preventing the knowledge from receding into history (becoming forgotten with the passage of time) and becoming tacit, including knowledge that had been tacit (e.g., taken for granted as a routine) before conversion into artifacts. The Meta-Artifact preserves the problem space (requirements for the domain) and solution space (systems satisfying the requirements) (see Glossary, problem space and solution space).

When breakdowns occur (see Glossary), stakeholders use the integrated modeling tools to create a view of the Meta-Artifact [41] to obtain understanding (see the Active Semantic Chain section) of the background for the explicit knowledge they have and of the routines they perform against the background.

Impact on Problem and Solution Space Gaps

The Meta-Artifact eliminates the gap (not necessarily missing requirements, but potentially a cause of the gap) between the problem space and the solution space. Rather than being disconnected, as generally described in the literature [e.g., 15,67], they are different views of the Meta-Artifact. This at first would seem to contradict the problem-space focus of Domain Rules Analysis. However, because of the initial comprehensive focus on the problem space, the frameworks and patterns of the Meta-Artifact (viewed as part of the solution space) would be derived independently of the solution space (see Figure 4.1). The Meta-Artifact, when applied through MAP, extends the modeling concept that the model is the application [52] by applying the concept to entire domains. The Meta-Artifact also extends the particulars of the concept beyond that of automatically generating code from the visual model (the basis for saying that the model is the application). That is, automatic code generation is just one of the subqualities noted for the Meta-Artifact (see Properties, Qualities, and Capabilities— Detailed Discussion).

The electronic linking of the artifacts in the Meta-Artifact is comprehensive in the sense that the source code for software links all of the statements required to generate the executable code. Just as it is possible to corrupt the source code in some way that would break its linkage to the current executable code, it would be possible to break the global linkage within the Meta-Artifact. However, *MSW* assumes the use of tools at least as powerful as those used for the prototype, including tools for requirements and configuration management, that with reasonable care would ensure that the artifacts of the Meta-Artifact were synchronized from the highest-level semantics through the running system. The procedure described in the Step Summary section includes steps to ensure the traceability among the artifacts, through successive iterations.

The Meta-Artifact includes the running system and the artifacts from which it is generated. This allows MAP to use the Meta-Artifact to automatically generate the software code for the running system from the electronically linked artifacts, directly from certain graphical representations and other code, which in turn are electronically linked to the other artifacts. The artifacts are changed in order to generate changes in the running system, so they always reflect the current running system, eliminating gaps between the problem and solution spaces. This is related to qualities such as stakeholder access to views of interest (see Glossary, stakeholder view).

Steps 14 and15 of the Step Summary include the identification of repeated patterns.

Need for Special-Purpose Views

A stakeholder's view of the system is not a single, static representation of a portion of the system or even the entire system that might have been prepared especially for the stakeholder (see Figure 3.4). In MAP, the stakeholder views are based on the actual system and can be changed in real time, as the stakeholder watches. The difference would be analogous to that between a sketch of the facade of a building prepared for an investor (stakeholder) during the early planning stages and the investor's standing at a selected location and looking at the facade of the completed building, then moving around and into the building, changing the investor's views in real time. The building in this analogy would correspond to the aspects of the Meta-Artifact that allow stakeholders to have different views of the current running system, and to change those views in real time. The building itself, however, would not provide the equivalent of all that the Meta-Artifact would provide, such as blueprints for the building or the goods and services that would be produced within it. The Meta-Artifact, on the other hand, includes the detailed specifications (blueprints) for building the running system, as well as the running system, which in turn can produce any of its outputs. This property is also related to the quality of providing stakeholder access to views of interest.

Multiple views with a common representation are provided by the UML and the integrated modeling tools. With strong tool support, the Meta-Artifact embodies the system architecture [41] and becomes a database for all information about the system (see Figure 2.1). The architecture embodied in the Meta-Artifact provides the unifying vision and guiding principles for the Meta-Artifact's structure (form) and behavior (function), so that it relates to the set of all artifacts of the system as a metamodel relates to the concepts of a domain [54]: the Meta-Artifact provides the rules and structure for its own continued development (see Glossary, Meta-Artifact).

Results of Key Properties, Qualities, and Capabilities—Detailed Discussion

Unifying Vision

The unifying vision provided by the architecture contributes to the unifying property of the Meta-Artifact. This unifying aspect of the Meta-Artifact, facilitated by the integrated modeling tools and the UML, assures coherent semantics throughout the Meta-Artifact—from individual elements of simple artifacts through complex artifacts of structures and collaborations—again paralleling a metamodel [54]. This semantic coherence is important because the common syntax, naming consistency, and common representation enforced by UML-based tools are not sufficient to provide coherent semantics throughout the system—without the architecture, different parts and views of the system might seem disconnected. For example, the use of repeated patterns in different parts of the system serves to unify it by greatly reducing the cognitive difficulty in understanding what those parts do [78]. Otherwise, the situation shown in Figure 3.3 occurs, where both components A and B provide the same service, but with different patterns. Developers and other stakeholders would need to interpret two different patterns for

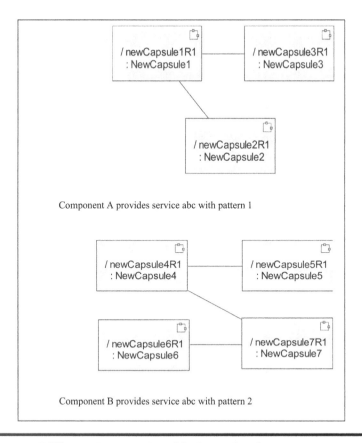

Figure 3.3   Different Patterns Provide Same Service.

the same service, roughly doubling the effort that would be required if the same pattern were used by both components.

Special-Purpose Views

The electronically linked and electronically stored artifacts that comprise the Meta-Artifact are available to provide documentation in various forms to support, for example, Integrated Product Development Systems (IPDSs), Capability Maturity Models (CMMs), or to produce any of the viewpoints defined by the DoD Architecture Framework Version 2.02 [20]. Stakeholders can obtain such special-purpose views (see Glossary) as byproducts, not directly required to produce the system, without requiring separate overhead functions or introducing delays.

The integrated modeling tools[1] extract artifacts from the database in which the Meta-Artifact resides (see Figure 2.1) using the active links among the artifacts to automatically generate the desired special-purpose artifacts[2] (see [58] for examples of automatically generated DoDAF artifacts). An overview of the process is shown in Figure 3.4.

Producing special-purpose views without separate overhead activities is not only a significant cost savings, but strongly supports the philosophy of letting developers be developers. Separate overhead activities and delays introduce direct costs

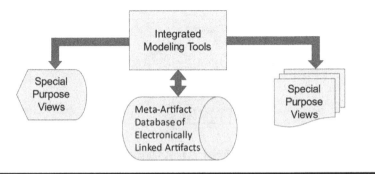

Figure 3.4   Special-Purpose Views.

and they also introduce the risk of indirect costs through artifacts that misrepresent the actual system.

Letting developers be developers increases the likelihood that artifacts will be produced timely and properly. This is part of the new way of thinking about the system encouraged by MAP (see Chapters 2 and 3). Because the Meta-Artifact, residing in its database, is the system, work done on it via any of its views is not just a throwaway activity for communication purposes. Conversely, only those views that are an integral part of the system need be generated by developers (consistent with [20]); other views may be generated through the tools as requested, even by non-developer stakeholders. As byproducts, they do not take on a life of their own as often happens with large systems or organizations when development processes must be bureaucratically enforced. Generation of views (or viewpoints) consistent with agile methods would be accommodated without tailoring.

If developers can benefit from a view, regardless of which stakeholder originated the view, as they produce the system (or the Meta-Artifact for MAP), with no need to stop to perform an overhead activity, they can produce the view without interrupting the process of building the system. If views that do not serve developers in this way but that are needed by other stakeholders can be prepared as byproducts, the process of building the system is likewise not interrupted or weakened through resource or schedule contention. Electronic artifacts, created and managed by integrated modeling tools, make this possible.

Visual Verification and Validation

Once the stakeholders agree that the visual model accurately captures the requirements, the Meta-Artifact carries the consistent UML representation through to the code [13,14,67], by using tools that generate the software code from the model [e.g., 38]. Because the automatically generated software code is one of the electronically linked artifacts, stakeholders can observe not only the static model but also the animated visual model as it is animated by the executing code, allowing stakeholders to literally see that the code is doing what they intended (similar to a spreadsheet, likely to be familiar to many users), providing visual verification and validation (VV&V) that it is doing the right thing right [1]. Further, the running code supports analysis to assess how well the system architecture meets nonfunctional performance requirements. Even the look and feel of the system can be assessed early, through stakeholder interaction with prototypes as they evolve across multiple iterations. Such VV&V reinforces the global consistency imposed by the tools (see Chapter 3 and Figure 2.1), in that stakeholders can see not only how the developers have interpreted their requirements, but also those of other stakeholders.

This VV&V capability is amplified by the iterative, incremental methods in MAP. That is, stakeholders can apply this technique from the earliest stages of development, to avoid costly mistakes later. The value of early agreement among the stakeholders on what the system is to do and whether it is doing it well is described in [50]. VV&V contributes to the unifying property of the Meta-Artifact by allowing stakeholders to see that the system is, or is not, doing what they wanted it to do. Through application of VV&V during successive iterations, VV&V helps assure consistency between stakeholder requirements and the system during the system's full lifecycle.

After a system is implemented, the visual model—always electronically connected to the running code—can be used for adapting the system to changing needs and technology in the current domain or extending it for an evolving domain (see Figure 4.1). This adaptation might include hypothesizing potential further improvements. Generating the code from the visual model, after it has passed VV&V, contributes to reliability throughout the lifecycle of the target systems.

Process and Product Are Different Views Rather than Separate Things

Related to producing specialized views as byproducts, all activities performed by developers on the electronically linked artifacts lead directly to the objective system, through the unifying and prescriptive (the code generated is the code that will be executed for operations) properties. The executable increment generated for each iteration ensures that new artifacts in the Meta-Artifact are linked with previous ones, both through the compiling performed by the tools and the VV&V performed by the stakeholders as part of continuous integration and delivery or deployment. The compiling of the artifacts to generate an executable increment provides a comprehensive linking of the artifacts in the same sense that source code statements for software are comprehensively linked to the executable code generated from the source code statements. The comprehensive linking of artifacts in the Meta-Artifact, in turn, makes them consistent with each other in the manner that source code statements are consistent with each other. The executable increments directly support continuous integration and delivery or deployment.

This unification of what has been in practice a troublesome disconnect [15, 67] between the problem space and the solution space (see the Impact on Problem and Solution Space Gaps section) results from the automatic creation and linking of the elements of the artifacts of the Meta-Artifact, as MAP is applied. The updated elements of the artifacts are stored in the database (see Figure 2.1) from which the tools can compose them into specialized products.

■ Conversely, all changes to the objective system also change the electronically linked artifacts (this is not necessary, nor is it preferred, as the objective system can be regenerated by first changing the higher-level artifacts of the Meta-Artifact).

■ From either direction, the active linking and integrated modeling tools preserve the current and unifying properties of the Meta-Artifact.

Active Semantic Chain

The active semantic chain for the system consists of the highest-level semantics of the system—requirements articulated as artifacts (e.g., requirements captured in use cases) electronically connected through successive electronic links in the chain (e.g., analysis and artifacts such as class and collaboration diagrams) to the lowest-level semantics of the executable components (e.g., software code) and their outputs. It is created by the integrated modeling tools, linking the electronically stored artifacts and their elements (e.g., a class or association in a class diagram or a message in a collaboration diagram), with the executable components and building on the semantics of the common representation provided by the UML. Embodied in the Meta-Artifact, the active semantic chain preserves the semantics of the system, from its genesis to its retirement. These semantics of the system are available as explicit knowledge, by application of the integrated modeling tools to the Meta-Artifact (e.g., by creating views appropriate to the stakeholder's current purpose). Access to electronically linked artifacts, in a single repository (see Figure 2.1), for all systems in a domain avoids the documentation-related problems described in [18], which describes the difficulty in establishing and maintaining links for documentation in current practice.

Using the Meta-Artifact, the active semantic chain provides bidirectional narratives (see Glossary, narratives)—both to articulate what stakeholders know explicitly and to trace back to the rationale for what they know implicitly (experience-related knowledge or common sense that are tacit, or background, knowledge).

The active semantic chain is at the core of the Meta-Artifact's ability to promote understanding of the system and continuous integration. A key aspect of this understanding is documentation that is always current, readily accessible, and represented from the stakeholders' viewpoint (see [74]) for impact of current documentation on semantics). Such documentation has been the dream and the nightmare of systems development since the first question about how a system worked. The integrated modeling tools provide views tailored to the interests of stakeholders, based on all of the artifacts from which the current running system is derived, giving the stakeholders convenient access to documentation that is far more comprehensive than what is likely to be available in current practice.

A key byproduct of the active semantic chain is comprehensive traceability. Within a view, a stakeholder can navigate from any artifact to artifacts of higher- or lower-level semantics (or from coarser to finer granularity) to assist in understanding, verifying, or validating the system. This traceability would also assist developers in gauging the impact of a change, including one related to hypothesizing. The value of determining the impact of changes to the system is explained clearly in [6].

The failures to elicit and translate requirements are worsened by tacit knowledge. The Meta-Artifact converts tacit knowledge into artifacts and preserves the knowledge of the system and embeds it in the system (see [79] regarding undocumented semantics residing in software code and human consciousness) as explicit knowledge, accessible through the active semantic chain, preventing the knowledge from receding into history (becoming forgotten with the passage of time) and becoming tacit (see Glossary, tacit knowledge).

Eliminate Temporal and Semantic Gaps—Detailed Discussion

Far from providing an active semantic chain such as that in MAP, traditional development artifacts produced for one phase may not be understandable to developers in another phase— e.g., designers may prepare entity relationship diagrams that coders misinterpret because they are unfamiliar with the representation and semantics, or the coders may write programs the designers cannot read. The interaction among developers tends to be limited to the handoffs from one phase to the next. The result is that each developer or development group has a narrowly focused responsibility. Breakdowns occur when developers for a phase try to apply the knowledge and routines (see Glossary, routines) of their disciplines against a tacit background that differs from that of the preceding discipline (see Glossary, background). That is, the explicit knowledge as well as the tacit knowledge (see Glossary, explicit and tacit knowledge) of the disciplines differs (Figure 3.5).

In practice, development projects do not comply with [41], which recommends having a single system architecture. Rather

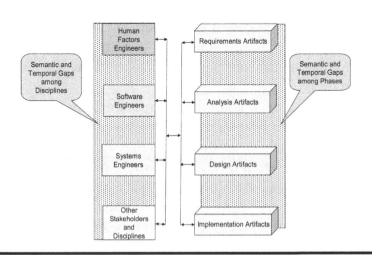

Figure 3.5   Gaps in Current Practice.

than separate architectures for each discipline, such as hardware and software, developers should have their respective views of the same system architecture, e.g., a hardware view or a software view. Separate architectures widen the semantic gaps among disciplines by adding differences based on architecture, such as different sets of guiding principles and different visions instead of a unifying vision for the system (see the Architecture Centricity section). The breakdowns caused by such architectural gaps are likely to involve substantial rework, in addition to breakdowns caused by the other disconnects independently of architectural gaps. The problem of disparate architectures is amplified when multiple systems in a domain must interact with each other, but are not based on a single domain architecture (see the Domain Rules Analysis section).

Notes

1 The tools used by *MSW* are object-oriented. Structured Analysis and Object-Oriented Analysis are the two most widely used development methods; both methods have evolved over decades [67,68].
2 The resulting artifacts may use UML icons or equivalent domain-specific icons, e.g., DoDAF icons. Generally, the artifacts of interest for special-purpose views are at the analysis level, but the Meta-Artifact database contains all of the artifacts down to the running system, if some special view of them is desired. My experience is that customers are fully prepared to accept equivalent representations or provide their own preferred icons.

Chapter 4

Domain Rules Analysis

The purpose of Domain Rules Analysis is to provide a practical method to clearly define and focus on an entire domain as the problem space, rather than a single application within the domain. The emphasis is on defining the problem space before moving to the solution space. To achieve this emphasis, Domain Rules Analysis considers three sources of Domain Rules: primary, supplemental, and other. Primary and supplemental sources are almost entirely about the problem space. For example, a primary source would be an official or formal definition of the domain (such as AIS or C4ISR; Figures 7.1 and 7.2), provided by a trade group, a major user, or academia. An example of a supplemental source would be the equivalent, but only for a subdomain (such as Purchasing or Battle Management). Other sources, such as an RFP or internal request, would likely include considerable solution-oriented information. Examples from all three sources are covered more extensively in [58].

A domain, according to the *American Heritage Dictionary*, is a sphere of activity, concern, or function; a field. In systems engineering, domains may be vertical, such as a full range of applications for a particular type of business or weapon

  DOI: 10.1201/9781003448891-4

systems for the Department of Defense, or horizontal, such as accounting, office automation, middleware for distributed objects, or operating systems, providing support to many vertical domains. Combinations or subsets of these vertical and horizontal classifications are also commonly viewed as domains (examples are covered more extensively in [58]).

Domain Rules Analysis and Related Technologies—Detailed Discussion

Domain Rules Analysis adds Domain Rules (see Domain Rules—Detailed Discussion) to two established methods, Domain Analysis [3,45,74] and Object-Oriented Domain Analysis (OODA) [15, 29, 34, 56]. Two persistent problems in applying both Domain Analysis and OODA have been the lack of a practical way to define the boundaries of a domain and to stay focused on its problem space without moving too quickly to the solution space of the domain. Domain rules make these two problems different sides of the same coin. Fully addressing the requirements for the rules that define the domain ensures a complete analysis of the solution space (see Table 3.3, Capability 1; also see Chapter 7).

As implied, OODA uses OOT [15,29,34,56,68]. OOT provides a structure for commonality and variability through inheritance, encapsulation, and polymorphism. Because of its inherent features, OOT for software allows a fuller realization of Domain Analysis than parameter and table-driven techniques (see the Frameworks and Other Benefits to Justify Domain Rules Analysis section). Domain Rules Analysis, building on OODA, uses OOT to make frameworks and patterns (see Glossary, framework, pattern; [15,30]) for the domain identified by Domain Rules. Objects derived from the framework as components can be composed into target systems [33,35], e.g., for product lines [23], using integrated modeling tools, applying

Table 4.1   Extensions and Enablers

Eight Elements of the Meta-Artifact Process (MAP)	
Extensions	Enablers
Meta-Artifact	Object-Oriented Technology (OOT)
Domain Rules Analysis	Visual Modeling with the Unified Modeling Language
Bifurcated Architecture	Integrated Modeling Tools (MDD)
	Architecture Centricity
	Iterative, Incremental Methods

and identifying useful patterns. Encapsulation expands the use of patterns [30] both at a design and at an architectural level by allowing discrete services to be bundled for reuse in multiple patterns (see Tables 4.5 and 4.6).

Some integrated modeling tools (e.g. [38]) greatly expand the composing of target systems by generating code from the framework for inter-process communication, creating concurrent, distributed, real-time applications with publish and subscribe interfaces (see [58] for an implementation discussion). Another feature of OOT, encapsulation, facilitates the inter-process communication by enabling interaction of components strictly based on services available through the publish-and-subscribe interfaces. See [58] for an extensive discussion of combining OODA with Domain Rules to form Domain Rules Analysis and using integrated modeling tools to generate code for inter-process communication (see Table 4.1).

Practical Considerations for Domain Rules Analysis

A focus on existing, planned, or preconceived solutions may limit the analysis of the domain in ways that defeat the purpose of Domain Rules Analysis, e.g.:

- Little *a priori* consideration of future systems
- Systems that are not adaptable (see Glossary, adaptability) within the current domain
- Systems that are not extensible (see Glossary, extensibility) for domain evolution
- Systems with extensive options that may never be used, rather than frameworks and patterns for composing target systems tailored for selected requirements

There are several assumptions implicit in domain analysis theory combined with OOT:

- A domain can be identified
- There are groups of applications within a domain with more commonality than differences
- Frameworks can be built by mapping from the problem space to appropriate classes
- Design patterns can be derived from the frameworks
- Applications in the solution space can be composed from the frameworks and patterns

In order to justify the effort required by Domain Rules Analysis, an organization would have to see a need to provide a domain-wide framework—"… an abstract design … in the form of a set of classes" [15]—along with patterns to satisfy its internal plans, a perceived market, or some combination. The organization would then have to invest substantially in the development, helping to explain why such a complete domain solution is uncommon.

Even with the natural support that OOT gives domain analysis in principle, there is a practical contradiction. The goal of domain analysis is to consider an entire domain (the problem space), but as Cohen [15] observes, object-oriented frameworks and patterns have tended to be connected to the solution space. This is an example of how domain analysis has relied in practice on defining the problem space from the solution space, e.g., extracting requirements from existing systems through reverse engineering. The dynamics of this practice and how to avoid it are discussed in the Application of Domain Rules section, so that the frameworks and patterns are derived independently of the solution space (see Figure 4.1).

Domain Rules—Detailed Discussion

Domain rules represent those aspects of a domain that seldom change, unlike business rules (see Table 4.7), but they may drive business rules in that business rules must comply with domain rules. Domain Rules provide the ability to set the boundaries of a domain independently of existing systems and the solution space in general. Domain Rules Analysis, using domain rules, provides a practical means to focus on the problem domain, with the goal of achieving a thorough analysis of the problem space to produce frameworks likely to cover the entire domain [15,34,67,68,3]. Domain rules (see Tables 4.2 and 4.3) are based on the underlying principles, theory, long-standing practices, or traditions of a domain, such as:

- Economic theory
- Laws of physics
- Principles of war
- Military doctrine
- Legal precedent
- Legislation
- Industry standards and practices

Domain Rules are used in conjunction with business rules (see Business Rules and Volatile Variability—Detailed Discussion) to produce a Bifurcated Architecture (see the Bifurcated Architecture section).

Table 4.2   AIS Domain Rules

Domain Rule	Prescriptive Description
Duality	Offset each increment to resources with a corresponding decrement, and vice versa. Characterize increments by transferring in (purchases and cash receipts) and the corresponding decrements by transferring out (sales and cash disbursements) [53].
Accounting equation	Ensure Assets = Liabilities + Owner's Equity
Income equation	Ensure Revenues – Expenses = Net Income (or Net Loss)
Accounting period	Ensure transaction effective date between accounting period end date and accounting period begin date
Accrual	Calculate portion of expense or revenue attributable to this accounting period, based on when the corresponding purchase or sale event occurred, not when cash is received or disbursed
Realization	Recognize when the expense occurred based on when the physical item or service was received
Matching	Match revenue that occurred in the accounting period with associated expenses
Money measurement	Provide a common unit of measure for all calculations by translating all measurements into monetary units
Entity	Define the boundaries of the organization for which accounts are kept and reports are made
Going concern	Prepare financial reports based on the assumption that the organization will continue its current operations indefinitely, not based on current liquidation value

(continued)

Table 4.2   (Continued)

Domain Rule	Prescriptive Description
Cost	Value assets based on original cost, not current value and not adjusted for inflation or deflation (i.e., using only monetary units attributed to the purchase at the time of purchase)
Consistency	Do not change the accounting method for a kind of event or asset from one accounting period to the next in order to enhance comparability of accounting reports from period to period
Conservatism	Recognize revenues and gains slower than expenses and losses
Materiality	Do not measure or record events that are insignificant, applying consistency and conservatism in determining significance [10, pp. 1–8, 1–11]

The mechanism used by which Domain Rules identify the boundaries of a domain is to establish what must be in the domain (in the sense of completeness—see Step Summary, steps 7 and 12) and what should be excluded. By this mechanism of inclusion or exclusion, domain rules serve to differentiate one domain from another and provide a reference baseline of the minimum requirements for the domain. For example, does ensuring that debits and credits are in balance (see Table 4.2) apply to military domains (see Figure 7.1)? Does placing the enemy in a position of disadvantage through the flexible application of combat power apply to AISs (see Figure 7.1)? Some domain rules might apply to multiple domains—of interest for reuse across multiple domains—e.g., prepare clear, uncomplicated plans and concise orders or directions to ensure thorough understanding (see Table 4.3). Such differentiation and the possibility of multiple domains

Table 4.3 C4ISR Domain Rules

Domain Rule	Prescriptive Description
Set the objective	Direct every military mission toward a clearly defined, decisive, and attainable objective. Commanders direct the use of available combat power toward clearly defined, attainable, and decisive goals. *The proper objective ("purpose") in battle is the destruction of the enemy's combat forces. To do this, however, subordinate commanders must be given "terrain objectives" toward which they move.*
Take the offensive	Seize, retain, and exploit the initiative. Offensive action is the most effective and decisive way to attain a clearly defined common objective.
Mass the effects	Mass the effects of synchronizing the employment of overwhelming combat power at the decisive place and time to gain the objective. *Achieve military superiority at the decisive place and time. Mass in this sense does not mean more men. Military superiority can be attained against a more numerical enemy if you have superiority in such things as weapons, leadership, morale, and training. Mass is generally gained by maneuver.*
Use forces economically	*Employ all combat power available in the most effective way possible to gain the objective; allocate essential combat power to secondary efforts. Allocate to secondary efforts minimum essential combat power. This is a misleading term because it does not mean what it sounds like. It does not mean do the job with minimum combat power. Note that the principle pertains to secondary efforts, and it is the means by which a superior general achieves mass as defined above. Mass and economy of force are on opposite sides of the same coin.*

(continued)

Table 4.3 (Continued)

Domain Rule	Prescriptive Description
Maneuver combat power	*Place the enemy in a position of disadvantage through the flexible application of combat power. Position your military resources to favor the accomplishment of your mission. Maneuver in itself can produce no decisive results, but if properly employed it makes decisive results possible through the application of the principles of the offensive, mass, economy of force, and surprise. It is by maneuver that a superior general defeats a stronger adversary.*
Use unity of command	*Designate a single decision maker responsible for all activities related to an operation. Focus all activity upon a single objective.*
Be secure	Never permit the enemy to acquire an unexpected advantage. *Another definition would be to take all measures to prevent surprise. A unit in bivouac, for example, uses outposts and patrols for security.*
Use surprise	Strike the enemy at a time, at a place, or in a manner for which he is unprepared. *Accomplish your purpose before the enemy can effectively react. Tactical or strategic surprise does not mean open-mouthed amazement. Thus, a corps may be surprised by an attack it has seen coming for several hours if this attack is too powerful for it to resist by itself and if no other unit is within supporting distance.*
Use simplicity	Prepare clear, uncomplicated plans and clear, concise orders to ensure thorough understanding.

with common domain rules would be useful in searching for reusable components from one domain to another. That is, applicable domain rules could be used to include components for consideration or exclude them from continued interest.

Table 4.4 Commonality, Stable Variability, and Volatile Variability

Category	Commonality	Variability	
		Stable	Volatile
Business rules			X
Domain Rules	X	X	

Domain rules form the overarching category of requirements that characterize a domain by distinguishing it (and the systems that meet the needs for the domain) from other domains. The function of domain rules in characterizing the domain would be consistent with the importance of cohesiveness in problem domains [3]. Domain rules serve as meta-rules that govern what subordinate categories of requirements are appropriate for the domain. In this way, domain rules are constraints. Examples of domain rules for the two domains considered in *MSW* are listed in Table 4.2 (referred to as accounting concepts in [10]) and Table 4.3 (Nine Principles of War from various sources).

As noted (see the Domain Rules—Detailed Discussion section), domain rules are stable over time, in contrast to business rules. Domain rules are unlikely to change over the entire life of the system, whereas business rules may change frequently over the system's life. Given this dichotomy between domain rules and business rules, domain rules are unlikely to ever become business rules or vice versa. Table 4.4 relates domain rules and business rules to commonality, stable variability, and volatile variability.

Application of Domain Rules

Domain rules are the invariant rules for a domain. That is, all applications (systems) for the domain must take account of the domain rules to determine which apply. Not all domain rules apply to every application of a domain, but each application must incorporate at least one of the domain rules in order to belong to the domain. The differences in domain rules applicable to systems in the domain reveal a partitioning of the domain through stable variability.

Domain Rules Analysis keeps MAP focused on the problem space (domain) by identifying domain rules (see Step Summary, steps 1.3 and 4–8), analysis classes [9] (see steps 9–16), and use cases to which the requirements can be allocated (see Step Summary), independently of the solution space. Use cases are problem oriented by definition, dealing with the requirements (explicit statements of needs) as the independent variables of the problem space, reinforcing the problem-oriented focus of Domain Rules Analysis.

Once the domain has been analyzed to provide sufficient completeness to adequately meet all stakeholders' needs, capability 4 (see Table 3.3) requires the construction of prescriptive instructions to implement the requirements for volatile variability and maintain the integrity of the prescriptive instructions over the complete lifecycle of the system if breakdowns occur or requirements change. The artifacts stored as information for capability 1 (see Table 3.3) must be related so as to provide a valid and accessible understanding of the stakeholders' requirements whenever they are converted to active knowledge during the complete lifecycle of the system, including all of the phases of development, regardless of which discipline is creating or using the artifacts (capability 2).

This again involves the lifecycle-centric systems development process, with emphasis on three persistent and closely related problems in software development technology (inadequate software reuse, reliability, and interoperability) that affect iterative and incremental system lifecycle integrity, development time, and cost. Domain Rules Analysis also identifies domain patterns, as described in Tables 4.5 and 4.6.

Steps 14 and 15 of the Step Summary include the identification of repeated patterns.

Table 4.5 Standard Accounting Cycles (Patterns)

Cycle Name	Description
Cash payments	Supplier or vendor invoice, receiving report, written check
Cash receipts	Customer checks and remittance advices
Payroll	Time cards, paychecks
Production	Materials requisition, labor time cards, production order, operations list
Facilities	Documents supporting the purchase of property, plant, and equipment
General ledger	Adjusting, closing, and correcting entries and input from various feeder cycles, e.g., expenditure and sales
Financing	Capital raising, e.g., bank notes, bond agreements, common stock issuances
Investment	Stocks, bonds, CDs, repurchase agreements
Purchasing	Purchase requisition, purchase order
Sales	Customer order, customer purchase order, bill of lading invoice

Table 4.7 lists the definitions that will be used.

Stable variability would be a secondary source of reuse. By factoring out volatile variability (see Business Rules and Volatile Variability—Detailed Discussion), and specializing domain rules, stable variability would potentially be applicable to multiple applications within a domain with little further specialization. Stable variability would be a source for distinguishing one application in the domain from another, but it would not be a source of volatility. For example, the choice of a depreciation method for a category of capital assets would be a business rule, subject to relatively frequent change based on regulations and policy. However, the code implementing a depreciation method—stable variability—is highly unlikely to change.

Table 4.6   Basic C2 Patterns

Name	Description
Plan	Translation of higher commander's vision/intent into specific Courses Of Action (COAs) in a compressed plan cycle for preparation and execution by subordinate elements. Define battle space areas of operation for synchronization and control. Generate alternative courses of action and evaluate against most likely and dangerous adversary actions. Develop synchronized schedule of tasks and activities for subordinates to prepare and execute. Develop integrated, combined effect operations plan to include all the battlefield functional areas.
Prepare	Outline activities by the unit before executing, to improve its ability to conduct the planned operation, including plan refinement, force protection, rehearsal, reconnaissance, integration and coordination of warriors and resources, inspections, and movement to planned locations.
Execute	Apply combat power to accomplish the planned mission, exercise control through assessment of battlespace to understand the situation in order to make execution and adjustment decisions for battle management.
Assess	Monitor and evaluate on a continuous basis throughout planning, preparation, and execution the current situation and progress of an operation and the evaluation of it against criteria of success to make decisions and adjustments.

Table 4.7   Business vs. Domain Rules

Business Rules	Domain Rules
Short term	Long term
Volatile (changing over time)	Stable (unchanging over time)
Driven by current business or mission context	Driven by application of a field of knowledge, such as accounting or command and control

Frameworks and Other Benefits to Justify Domain Rules Analysis—Detailed Discussion

While focusing on the problem space, Domain Rules Analysis provides a comprehensive analysis of the domain, using domain rules as a measure of completeness (the see Step Summary section, steps 7 and 12), ensuring that the requirements of the domain rules, at a minimum, have been identified and analyzed. During this comprehensive domain analysis, Domain Rules Analysis also categorizes requirements that represent volatile variability as business rules (see procedure steps 4, 7, 12, and 16). The Bifurcated Architecture requires that volatile variability be identified throughout the application of MAP (see Step Summary).

Figure 4.1 depicts the Domain Rules Analysis of the original domain (OD, or the second largest circle) to create a framework for the entire domain (see Domain Rules Framework in Figure 4.1). All of the particular solutions are derived as adaptations from the Domain Rules Framework, through specialization (by using OOT), the frameworks are divided into various class hierarchies (see Glossary, framework). The arrows in Figure 4.1 show this progression from problem space, to framework, to solution space graphically. The SE square represents the third solution. Individual solutions do not need to be generalized, because adaptation for reuse is achieved through the Domain Rules Framework.

The purpose of performing the Domain Rules Analysis would be to produce a framework for the domain that was sufficiently complete that new base classes would be needed only when the domain evolved (DE, or the largest circle). The proportion of derived classes available initially would depend on the domain and circumstances, such as priority applications, and funding. In a bifurcated architecture, once the stable (over time) domain framework and patterns (see Step Summary steps 1–3, 6, and 9) were made for a domain, specific applications would

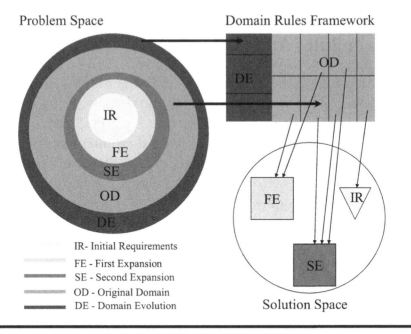

Figure 4.1   Domain Rules Analysis of Requirements.

be composed from components derived from the framework, guided by the patterns. Tailoring of applications could focus almost entirely on the business rules.

Because Domain Rules Analysis provides a process for performing a comprehensive examination of the domain, by applying it in close coordination with two of the capabilities of the enabling technologies—one for analysis and one for implementation—it can effectively address the needs of network-centric environments. The analytical capability is the collaboration diagram. The implementation capability is the integrated modeling tool support for publish and subscribe interfaces, which preserves the integrity of the collaboration analysis (see [58] for examples).

During development, Domain Rules Analysis can be used to systematically identify the interfaces required among the objects in their collaborations. Such a focus on the interfaces as well as the structural and behavioral elements of the domain would contribute significantly to the completeness of the Meta-Artifact.

Using Domain Rules Analysis to produce a Bifurcated Architecture systematically deals with both commonality and variability, as discussed in the next section. These two extensions (see Table 4.1) of MAP intersect. While Domain Rules Analysis leads to a framework for commonality from which stable variability can be derived through specialization, the Bifurcated Architecture goes farther by separating volatile variability from both commonality and stable variability.

Chapter 5

Bifurcated Architecture

The Bifurcated Architecture separates the volatile variability—business rules—from stable variability and commonality (see Glossary). Common definitions of business rules [e.g., 9] do not include volatile variability as a defining characteristic. Business rules have always been captured and analyzed with other requirements, whether implicitly or explicitly (see [58] for a detailed discussion). In a bifurcated architecture, developers would allocate the prescriptive rules implementing the business rules (see Tables 5.1 and 5.2) to an external repository (file or database; see Figure 5.1) where they can be maintained more efficiently and accurately than when they are embedded in code, because they are treated as data by the system. As external data, the business rules become more accessible for such purposes as analysis, audit, and training. In this way, the Bifurcated Architecture greatly simplifies adaptation in the current domain and extensibility in an evolving domain, because the features most likely to change—represented as business rules—can be easily modified, even in real time.

 DOI: 10.1201/9781003448891-5

Business Rules and Volatile Variability—Detailed Discussion

Business rules consist of two parts:

- Prescriptive statements whose purpose is to assure compliance with the business rules (see Table 5.1)
- Declarative statements that define or constrain some aspect of the business (see Glossary; [4,9,39,36,37,55]).

In government and business, operational compliance with budget policies or regulatory compliance with tax law would be examples of declarative business rules. In the military, rules of engagement such as use of armed force as a last resort or avoid harming civilians would be examples comparable to declarative business rules. See Tables 5.1 and 5.2 for the corresponding prescriptive instructions. For a diagrammatic representation of where business rules fit in the traditional management process, see Figure G.3.

More generally, business rules represent volatile variability—those aspects of the system that change relatively often, in contrast to the stability (and commonality in some cases) of domain rules and stable variability. References to business rules without explicitly specifying rules of engagement are intended to include rules of engagement.

Means of Identifying Business Rules

The concept of volatile variability provides a means of identifying business rules. Business rules are volatile because they change in response to such things as the current situation—e.g., environmental conditions, regulations, technology, knowledge, and attitudes. Unlike domain rules, a system's business rules are under the control of the organization that uses the system. They capture the organization's business

Table 5.1 Sample Business Rules for AIS

Business Rules	Prescriptive Instructions
Financial— Compliance with budget policies	If on approval of this request for purchase order, total encumbered dollars for this subsidiary ledger account would be greater than the budget for that account, reject the request.
Operational— Compliance with authorization polices	If the amount for this purchase order exceeds the signature authority of the buyer (purchasing agent), reject the purchase order.
Regulatory— Compliance with tax law and regulation	If the type of asset-type specified for this subsidiary ledger account does not match the asset type for this depreciation method, reject the transaction: either the wrong subsidiary ledger account is being used to set up this asset or the wrong depreciation method has been specified.
Fraud— Compliance with legal and policy requirements	Select all transactions for a specified subsidiary ledger account for a specified time period exceeding a specified dollar amount, then process the details of those transactions (e.g., name of vendor, name of purchasing agent, address of vendor, shipping address) through specified neural network to detect patterns of fraudulent activity.

philosophy and practices in terms "… that describe, constrain, and control the structure, operations, and strategy" of the organization [39]. Business rules may be derived from external sources that the organization does not control, such as domain rules, regulations, and cultural considerations. Such business rules reflect the organization's interpretations of how to comply with external sources. The organization's interpretation may change in terms of both how to comply and which external sources are relevant. To the extent that the external source is itself subject to change (e.g., frequently revised federal regulations), the volatility is increased.

Table 5.2   Sample Rules of Engagement as Business Rules

Rules of Engagement	*Prescriptive Instructions*
Use armed force as the last resort	When possible, the enemy will be warned first and allowed to surrender. Armed civilians will be engaged only in self-defense. Civilian aircraft will not be engaged without approval from above division level unless it is in self-defense.
Avoid harming civilians unless necessary to save US lives	If possible, try to arrange for the evacuation of civilians prior to any US attack. If civilians are in the area, do not use artillery, mortars, armed helicopters, AC-130s, tube- or rocket-launched weapons, or M551 main guns against known or suspected targets without the permission of a ground maneuver commander, LTC, or higher (for any of these weapons). If civilians are in the area, all air attacks must be controlled by a FAC or FO. If civilians are in the area, close air support (CAS), white phosphorus, and incendiary weapons are prohibited without approval from above division level. If civilians are in the area, do not shoot except at known enemy locations. If civilians are not in the area, you can shoot at suspected enemy locations.
Avoid harming civilian property unless necessary to save US lives	Public works such as power stations, water treatment plants, dams, or other utilities may not be engaged without approval from above division level. Hospitals, churches, shrines, schools, museums, and any other historical or cultural site will not be engaged except in self-defense.

(*continued*)

Table 5.2 (Continued)

Rules of Engagement	Prescriptive Instructions
Treat all civilians and their property with respect and dignity.	Before using privately owned property, check to see if any publicly owned property can substitute. No requisitioning of civilian property without permission of a company-level commander and without giving a receipt. If an ordering officer can contract for the property, then do not requisition it. No looting. Do not kick down doors unless necessary. Do not sleep in their houses. If you must sleep in privately owned buildings, have an ordering officer contract for it.
Control civilians engaged in looting	Senior person in charge may order warning shots. Use minimum force but not deadly force to detain looters. Defend Panamanian (and other) lives with minimum force including deadly force when necessary.
Secure and protect roadblocks, checkpoints, and defensive positions	Mark all perimeter barriers, wires, and limits. Erect warning signs. Establish second positions to hastily block those fleeing. Senior person in charge may order warning shots to deter breach. Control exfiltrating civilians with minimum force necessary. Use force necessary to disarm exfiltrating military and paramilitary. Attack to disable, not destroy, all vehicles attempting to breach or flee. Vehicle that returns or initiates fire is hostile. Fire to destroy hostile force. Vehicle that persists in breach attempt is presumed hostile. Fire to destroy hostile force. Vehicle that persists in flight after a blocking attempt IAW instruction 2b is presumed hostile. Fire to destroy hostile force.

Related to Table 5.1, see Step Summary steps 4 and 16 for identifying and allocating volatile variability (business rules or rules of engagement) .

Commonality and Variability

Volatile variability (see Table 4.4) supplements the customary definitions of business rules by placing business rules in the context of commonality and variability and aiding in their identification during all phases of the system's lifecycle. That is, developers and stakeholders can apply the criterion of volatility—frequency of change—to identify functions to be externalized (see Step Summary, step 16). The volatility criterion should make it unnecessary to have detailed definitions and rules for identifying business rules. While ultimately a matter of judgment as to whether the variability was volatile, the likely frequency of change would provide an objective measure. The frequency might vary from very often (e.g., hourly or daily for online sales or time-critical targeting) to a few times over the lifecycle of the system, but regardless of the exact frequency, when business rules do change, externalizing them avoids costly maintenance activities.

Business rules may apply to automated functions or people. If they applied to people, as would most Rules of Engagement, then they might affect the interfaces with supporting automated systems. Such automated support may be indirect, for example, decision support aids for calling in direct fires. Rules that typically apply to people could also form the basis for automated functions such as robotic behavior in combat, target identification in missiles, or weapon-target pairing in manned aircraft, with related use in data correlation and fusion algorithms.

Objective of Bifurcated Architecture—Detailed Discussion

The Bifurcated Architecture enhances the concepts of commonality and variability in two ways:

- Differentiating stable variability from volatile variability (see Glossary)
- Providing physical as well as logical separation (see Figure 5.1)

The logical and physical separation provided by the Bifurcated Architecture yields multiple benefits, including:

- Improved reliability by eliminating the need to change software code as is done when business rules or rules of engagement are not externalized
- Reduced maintenance costs by eliminating the need to change software code as is done when business rules are not externalized
- Increased visibility of the enterprise's business rules for internal control [32,58], consistency, financial audits, and security audits
- Increased reusability and interoperability by removing volatile variability from the software code in components, so that the components represent only commonality or stable variability
- Use by decision support tools

Coupled with Domain Rules Analysis, Bifurcated Architecture seeks to systematically and completely analyze a problem domain in a way that identifies its volatile variability along with other outcomes of the analysis, regardless of what the basic function, purpose, or aspect of the resulting components may be.

Architecture Neutrality

The Bifurcated Architecture is orthogonal to the system architecture. Apart from separating the volatile variability at the point of occurrence (see Figure 5.1), the architecture is unaffected. The architecture-centric MAP proceeds to identify an architecture that is most appropriate for the domain requirements—it is not driven by business rules, i.e., not business rules centric. The difference is fundamental and

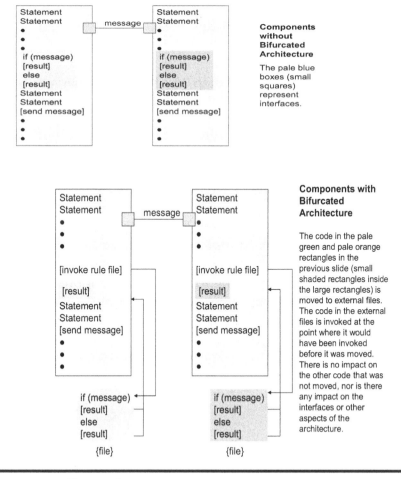

Figure 5.1   Bifurcated Component.

philosophical. MAP does not impose a particular architecture or specific design patterns. It starts at the beginning, with the problem space. MAP leads to architectural patterns (frameworks) and analysis patterns (collaborations) for the problem space. Design patterns would follow. A major concern of MAP is to avoid imposing solutions that have not been derived from the problem space. Once enough analysis work has been done to discern patterns for the problem space, developers would refer to sources of existing patterns to find matches. They would do the same for design. Figure 5.1 shows implementation views of the Bifurcated Architecture. Not all classes (or components) would have rules. In this sense, the Bifurcated Architecture extends OOT, by adding greater encapsulation for rules.

(Related to Figure 5.1, see step 16 of Step Summary, to separate volatile variability in all phases of development.)

Role of Object-Oriented Technology

Object-Oriented Technology facilitates separating business rules from the rest of an application in a decentralized manner for the Bifurcated Architecture, because the prescriptive rules implementing the business rules can be allocated to repositories (see Figure 5.1) corresponding to individual components, if appropriate for the architecture. The concept of the external business rule repository does not depend on a centralized database. Multiple databases for individual components would be an option. The defining characteristics of the Bifurcated Architecture are that prescriptive rules implementing business rules are:

■ Separated from program code, hardware logic, or something in between such as Field-Programmable Gate Arrays

- Accessible to all authorized stakeholders
- Changeable by all authorized stakeholders

See Domain Rules Analysis and Related Technologies—Detailed Discussion for a summary of these characteristics and the overall impact on systems development.

Chapter 6

Architecture Centricity

Architecture Centricity is an enabler and a well-established design principle. While the other MAP enablers are not highlighted to the same extent, Architecture Centricity is highlighted because of the particular emphasis it receives in MAP. The architecture should flow down to all that follows, providing guidelines, principles (e.g., architecture centricity), imperatives, and a unifying vision that are traceable through design and implementation because of the active semantic chain (see the Active Semantic Chain section). This broad purpose is included explicitly or implicitly in the standard definitions of architecture such as the following:

> The architecture of a system is a specification of the parts and connectors of the system and the rules for the interactions of the parts using the connectors [71].

Central Role of Architecture Centricity

Architectural ideas are made concrete in the design and code. If the architecture does not live apart from a particular

 DOI: 10.1201/9781003448891-6

architecture, it cannot serve the above purpose or the ISO definition [41]. Architecture provides the page for everyone to be on. Up to around 2010, progress in architecture centricity moved in the direction of this principle, but then divergent approaches emerged, e.g., technology stacks or solution architectures. An architecture must be adhered to if its central role is to be realized. Its major benefits derive from its being a stable reference point. If there is an architecture adopted by the development team, it should be followed. If the architecture is not adequate, then it should be officially changed, but not ignored. Among the benefits of adhering to an architecture are preserving architecture quality attributes and other design imperatives, such as OOT. Of particular interest in today's systems is cybersecurity. Any system can be hacked, but the likelihood is reduced if cybersecurity is a required architecture quality attribute from the outset. Combined with object-oriented concepts such as invariants and data hiding (see the Domain Rules Analysis and Related Technologies—Detailed Discussion section), this approach of insisting on architectural integrity and use of OOT assures that the desired level of cybersecurity is built into the system and preserved over the life of the system.

Technology-stacks or solution architectures tend to be retrospective (de facto) rather than prescriptive. That is, they do not qualify as architectures in the sense described earlier in this chapter. Nevertheless, the two can be complementary by using a prescriptive architecture to select and tailor a technology stack.

Consistent with the Unified Software Development Process [9], stakeholders do not start MAP with a preconceived architecture (e.g., a commercially available stack). Rather, the architecture emerges from the application of MAP. Architecture is part of the solution and MAP, through Domain Rules Analysis, which emphasizes thoroughly analyzing the problem space before moving to the solution space. Deriving the architecture through MAP allows the Meta-Artifact to recursively guide the process of making the architecture (and the rest of the domain analysis), while also embodying the architecture. MAP thus overcomes a common weakness of OODA in moving prematurely to the solution space (see Chapter 4) by using the Meta-Artifact to derive the architecture from the requirements.

Unifying Vision

Architecture provides a unifying vision and guiding principles for a system [6,9]. The unifying vision and guiding principles provide an overarching concept that should be captured in the architectural baseline, to lead all stakeholders to a common goal. Architecture focuses on the significant structural elements of a system, their relationships, externally visible properties, and interactions among them. The need for a strongly controlled architecture can be viewed as a major cross-functional requirement; it is a fundamental governance tool. For MAP, the guiding principles would include consistent application of the extensions and the other four enablers (see Table 4.1). The emphasis of architecture centricity on the global attributes of a system, and its guidance of the other enabling technologies (see Table 4.1, Enablers), is crucial to creating frameworks and patterns (see Glossary) and composability (assembling components into target systems [33,35]) of the Meta-Artifact.

The unifying vision of architecture is especially useful in applying agile methods. Individual use cases or groups of them can be selected and assigned for agile development (see Step Summary). Because the use cases are described in terms of the architecture, through standard interfaces with other use cases, they automatically conform to the architecture for the overall system. As part of the architecture, the use case will already have a schedule and structure that is consistent with those of the overall system. Applying use cases to agile methods has been done successfully and described in literature [42,59).

Process Implications—Detailed Discussion

By realizing architecturally significant use cases [948] in the early iterations (see [58] for further details) of development, stakeholders can agree on a stable architecture to provide an architectural baseline for governance that will avoid rework later, while fully accommodating adaptation and domain evolution (see Glossary, adaptability and extensibility and Figure 4.1). In this way, the architecture governs the significant structural elements and the collaborations among them during the lifecycle of the system. A solution-independent architecture provides an ontology for the solution space and a governance tool for its development and maintenance. To ensure that this happens requires adherence to the principle of architecture centricity.

Architecture centricity requires a process that preserves the integrity of the architecture and applies the architecture, as represented by the architectural baseline, for the entire lifecycle of the system. The problem-focused architecture that results from MAP differs from Enterprise Architectures in being fully separated from existing solutions, which include the existing organization for the domain. Further, multiple domains or organizations may be encompassed by a MAP architecture. That is, architecture centricity is adherence to a particular architecture; once it is captured in the baseline, changes to the baseline should be minimal [9]. Architecture centricity strongly supports the governance process and Domain Rules Analysis by providing a stable baseline as the analysis proceeds over many iterations and increments.

The formality of the UML, implemented with VSD tools (e.g., [38]), gives precise, unambiguous meaning to each of the elements of the architecture. The full realization of the architecture is embodied in the Meta-Artifact and is seen through the multiple views of the Meta-Artifact that are supported by the UML, which require the integrated modeling tools for practical application (see Figure 2.1). MAP encourages the concept of a single architecture for a system, with multiple views (such as those supported by the UML), as defined in [41], rather than multiple architectures. MAP also greatly improves the three persistent, nonfunctional qualities of reliability, reuse, and interoperability, which focus on the global attributes of a system and reduce lifecycle costs.

Chapter 7

Procedure to Apply MAP

The steps below, presented in a logical order for serial application, summarize the procedure, which is described in detail in [58]. Unless there is a statement to go back to a previous step for a given condition, the rule is to go to the next step. If there is a need to go back to a previous step n (e.g., because of accepting an alternative hypothesis), then the same rule applies after completing step n; proceed to step $n + 1$. However, there are opportunities for significant parallel and iterative application for teams of developers. Figure 7.3 shows the parallel and iterative nature of the procedure.

Step Summary

Each of the following steps may add artifacts to the Meta-Artifact or change existing artifacts. As the steps are repeated through successive iterations and as artifacts are created from other electronically linked artifacts within an iteration, the Meta-Artifact is applied recursively. See Figure 2.1 for how these steps, performed during the requirements and analysis activities

DOI: 10.1201/9781003448891-7

of each iteration, relate to the overall flow of MAP and the dynamic interaction of its eight elements.

1. Identify domain and extract its domain rules
    1.1 Determine explicit definitions of the domain from primary sources
    1.2 Extract domain rules (as requirements) and other requirements (including quality requirements) from the primary sources; apply knowledge management principles to identify any tacit requirements
    1.3 Identify use cases from the domain rules and requirements available at this point; identify use cases for agile development, if appropriate
2. Extract domain rules (as requirements) and other requirements (including quality requirements) from supplemental sources
    2.1 Identify the established subdomains (see Figure 7.1 for military examples, and Figure 7.2 for business examples), functions (or applications), methods, processes, procedures, and extract domain rules (as requirements) and other requirements (including quality requirements)
    2.2 Identify the established processing cycles, business processes, and patterns (see e.g., Table 4.5) and extract as domain rules (requirements) and other requirements (including quality requirements); apply knowledge management principles to identify any tacit requirements. Identify use cases from the domain rules and requirements available at this point. Identify use cases for agile development, if appropriate.
3. Extract domain rules (as requirements) and other requirements (including quality requirements) from other sources (e.g., from a request, solicitation, or stakeholder interviews); apply knowledge management principles to identify any tacit requirements. Identify use cases from

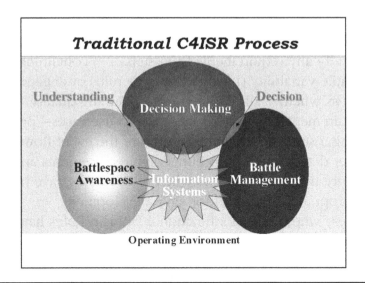

Figure 7.1   Traditional C4ISR Process Subdomains.

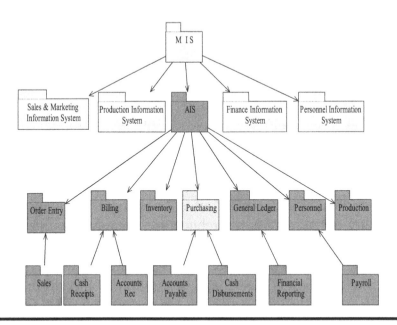

Figure 7.2   AIS Context.

the domain rules and requirements available at this point. Identify use cases for agile development, if appropriate.

4. Identify any requirements from steps 1–3 containing volatile variability (business rules or rules of engagement)

5. Assess whether all requirements (including quality requirements) have been allocated to use cases—preferably using a standard template to capture the event flows and other details such as nonfunctional requirements and ensure traceability; assess whether use cases have been appropriately allocated for agile development

6. Assess whether all nonfunctional Domain Rules have been allocated to all use cases that they affect, along with other nonfunctional requirements (such as quality attributes) for use-case realization during design and ensure traceability

7. Assess completeness by tracing all requirements, including nonfunctional requirements and volatile variability, to use cases

8. Decide whether to add or modify use cases in this or later builds or iterations. When using USDP or Rational Unified Process (RUP [11,48]), the decision to defer would be influenced by the current iteration and phase

   8.1 Add or modify use cases; identify results for agile development as appropriate

9. Identify analysis classes and create collaborations to realize the use cases and ensure traceability; use the collaborations to form alternative hypotheses for relationships among analysis classes. Assess architecture, comply or modify as appropriate.

10. Allocate requirements previously allocated to use cases to analysis classes and ensure traceability; form hypotheses for alternative allocations of requirements to analysis classes and update use cases and collaborations accordingly. Agree on the architecture or modifications to the architecture resulting from alternative hypotheses.

11. Allocate any nonfunctional domain rules to all analysis classes that they affect, along with other nonfunctional requirements (including quality attributes) for realization during design and ensure traceability
12. Assess completeness by tracing all requirements, including nonfunctional requirements and volatile variability, to analysis classes; form hypotheses for alternative allocations of requirements and relationships; update use cases accordingly
13. Decide whether to add or modify analysis classes in the current or a later build or iteration; update allocations, relationships, and hypotheses accordingly
14. Assess the analysis classes for commonality, e.g., patterns
    14.1 Decide whether to create application-specific, general, or service packages
    14.2 Create application-specific packages if no commonality
    14.3 Create application general packages if commonality, or
    14.4 Create service packages
15. Assess the analysis classes for stable variability, e.g., patterns
    15.1 Determine if optional or specific service packages
    15.2 Create application-specific classes if no stable variability
    15.3 Create optional service packages if stable variability
16. Asses analysis classes for volatile variability (business rules or rules of engagement) and allocate to an external repository for implementation. Begin next iteration at 1.

Diagram of Steps

Figure 7.3 is a graphical representation of the Step Summary using an activity diagram [8]. The description in each activity with a step number is abbreviated, but the step numbers correspond to the procedure described previously, for reference to a more detailed description of the step.

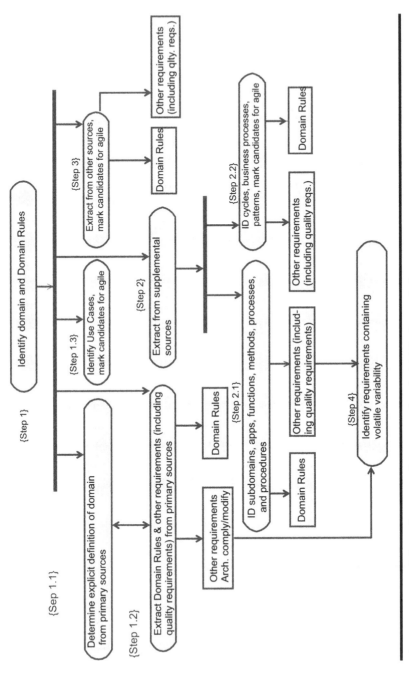

Figure 7.3   Activity Diagram of Steps to Apply MAP: Steps 1-4.

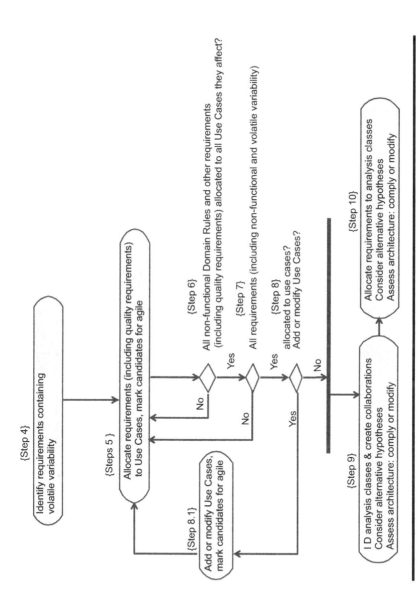

Figure 7.3   (Continued) Activity Diagram of Steps to Apply MAP: Steps 4-10.

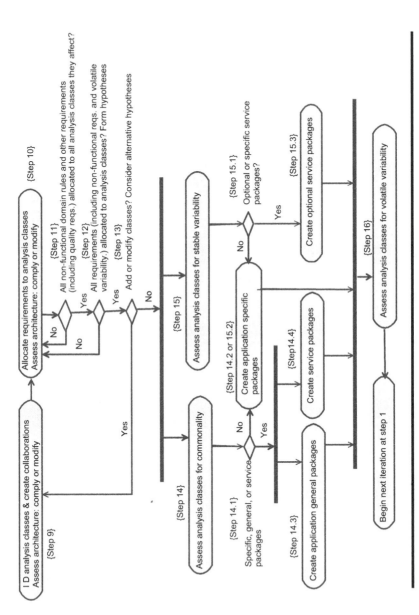

Figure 7.3   (Continued) Activity Diagram of Steps to Apply MAP: Steps 9-16.

Modeling Considerations in Applying the Procedure—Detailed Discussion

For distributed applications, sequence diagrams are especially useful for specifying inter-process communications [8, chapter 18]. The lifelines for each process (or passive classes used by the processes) then document what is to be accomplished within the classes (active classes for processes [9]) on the sequence diagram. Both actions and states can be shown visually and documented on the lifelines when using appropriate integrated modeling tools (e.g., [38]). When generating code, state machines ultimately implement the states and actions on these lifelines. Since code is not generated for the business rules, it is at this point that the design work for business rules would diverge from that for program code.

Sequence diagrams would remain useful for business rules, both for analyzing and for documenting them. Design and subsequent development workflows within each iteration would differ for business rules in that they would be transformed into production rules rather than program code, then maintained in a business rules database [39]. While state machines could still be useful to document the detailed logic within states and actions on a lifeline, activity diagrams would be more suitable for higher-level understanding (e.g., for nontechnical stakeholders), since the nature of such logic focuses on the activities that take place within an object rather than event-ordered behavior of an object [8, chapter 21].

Allocating the detailed logic to the states within a class provides a powerful organizing technique, at an even finer granularity than a class, useful for stakeholders with a low-level technical interest. The logic for an individual state can be highly cohesive as well as providing smaller chunks for understandability. Representing a class visually down to the granularity of individual states, combined with the externalized business rules, enhances understandability by leaving only a relatively small amount of total system logic to be realized solely in program code. As part of the active semantic chain, the enhanced understandability provided by the finer level of visual granularity when representing a class with state diagrams contributes significantly to the Meta-Artifact's quality of promoting understanding.

For a comprehensive prototype made with MAP and the procedure described earlier, see [58].

Chapter 8

Summary Review

MAP includes the following three extensions:

- Meta-Artifact
- Domain Rules Analysis
- Bifurcated Architecture

MAP combines these extensions with the following enabling technologies and methods:

- OOT
- Visual modeling with the UML
- Integrated modeling tools, including code generation, requirements management, database management, continuous integration and delivery or deployment, and configuration management
- Iterative, incremental methods
- Architecture centricity

DOI: 10.1201/9781003448891-8

Impact of MAP

MAP with its enabling extensions, and the infrastructure of the enabling technologies on which MAP depends, provides a complete process for making software-intensive systems (see Chapter 7). MAP addresses significant needs of highly integrated, software-intensive systems in network-centric environments. For a working example of the application of the complete MAP, see Prototype in [58].

The Meta-Artifact offers properties, qualities, and capabilities that help stakeholders and developers understand and reason about domain and target systems of interest. MAP, through the central role of the Meta-Artifact, and incorporating the view that a computer program is a hypothesis about the requirements, offers new ways to look at systems and their development, even changing the roles of developers and stakeholders (see [58] for a detailed discussion). By showing the common function of control in the management of enterprises in general, MAP suggests that it would apply to any domain involving such management activities.

Because it builds on mainstream technologies and concepts, MAP is ready for application by a wide range of practitioners, at least in the two domains discussed, but probably others as well. It is especially well suited to green-field projects, because of its domain-wide, problem space focus. This is an example of one of the fundamental and philosophical characteristics of MAP. MAP is a comprehensive process that uses rigorous analysis (based on current widely accepted methods, concepts, and best practices) to make an architecture that is appropriate for the domain. It does not impose a predetermined architecture (such as a multi-agent architecture) or pattern on a domain. It does the analysis first to determine what frameworks and patterns are appropriate, which does not preclude using existing ones. Rather than being brittle, MAP is open to changes in the enabling technologies on which it is based. Its unique concepts, such as Domain Rules and Volatile Variability, which underlie Domain Rules Analysis and Bifurcated Architecture, are independent of the particulars of the enabling technologies.

MAP accomplishes the following:

1. Comprehensively articulates stakeholders' explicit and tacit knowledge as narratives for conversion into development artifacts that are retained as information that can be converted back to active knowledge (see Glossary) to assure adequate understanding and proper implementation of needs during the complete lifecycle of the system

2. Reduces or eliminates the gaps among development disciplines and development phases during development, and among systems in a domain during operations and maintenance

3. Considers other existing systems and future systems in conjunction with the system under development because of both the explicit and tacit knowledge contained in the other systems, on which the system under development may depend, especially when they must interact with each other. This in turn requires a comprehensive consideration of the domain in which the systems reside.

4. Reduces the need to change software source code for maintenance resulting from breakdowns (see Glossary) or changing needs, with resulting reductions in costs and defects

Interaction of the Three Extensions

The Meta-Artifact is the electronically linked set of all of the artifacts of development, amplified by three extensions of MAP and five enabling technologies and the Meta-Artifact's recursive use in MAP for its own development.

The Meta-Artifact provides a knowledge management narrative across time for the artifacts of development for the domain. The Meta-Artifact continuously supplies the teleological remedy to the entropy that otherwise occurs with time, as development progresses and during operation and maintenance of the system, through its application in MAP, thereby converting knowledge captured in the Meta-Artifact into action and action into additional knowledge in the Meta-Artifact (see Glossary, Meta-Artifact and time).

Domain Rules Analysis uses a new concept, Domain Rules to help set the boundaries of the domain and, in conjunction with the Volatile Variability captured for the Bifurcated Architecture, to keep the focus on the problem domain. Domain Rules Analysis, by assuring a comprehensive analysis of the problem domain before developing a solution, provides the completeness needed for the Meta-Artifact to represent the totality of the solution space, including frameworks, patterns, and components (see Glossary, framework and pattern) from which target systems can be specialized and composed.

The Bifurcated Architecture separates the Volatile Variability—represented by business rules—normally embedded in code, into an external database so that authorized users can directly change it (see Figure 5.1). The separation of stable commonality and variability from Volatile Variability in the Bifurcated architecture can be achieved through readily available COTS products. The externalization of the volatile variability in the form of business rules in distributed databases allows the volatile variability to be managed by end users (see Glossary). The combination of the three extensions contributes significantly to reuse, reliability, and interoperability, three persistent and closely related problems in software development (see Table 4.1 and Figure 2.1).

Architecture Centricity

Architecture Centricity provides a unifying vision and guiding principles for a system's structural elements and the collaborations among them (see the Architecture Centricity section; [6,9]). For MAP, the guiding principles would include consistent application of the extensions and enablers (see Table 4.1). MAP preserves the integrity of the architecture and applies it, as represented by the architectural baseline, for the entire lifecycle of the system (see Architecture Centricity section). MAP's architecture centricity strongly supports Domain Rules Analysis by providing a stable baseline as the analysis proceeds over many iterations and increments.

Changing Roles

MAP causes significant changes in the roles of stakeholders and developers (see [58] for a detailed assessment):

- Volatile variability managed by end users rather than developers
- Domain-wide, long-term focus for development of the first Meta-Artifact and its continued use through MAP
  - New target systems not a separate standalone activity
  - Manipulate current Meta-Artifact to produce new target systems
  - New target systems take account of future target systems
- Responsibility spans phases

Use entire active semantic chain with multiple views rather than multiple products related to time and discipline.

Glossary

All of the entries in this glossary define only how the terms are used in *MSW*, so there may be other definitions for these terms not included here. The symbol † indicates a new concept developed in [58].

Active semantic chain (†): consists of the highest-level semantics of the system—requirements articulated as artifacts electronically connected through successive links in the chain—e.g., analysis and design artifacts—to the lowest-level semantics of the executable components (e.g., software code) and their outputs. It is created by the integrated tools from the electronically stored artifacts, building on the semantics of the common representation provided by the UML. Embodied in the Meta-Artifact, the active semantic chain preserves the semantics of the system, from its genesis to its retirement.

Using the Meta-Artifact, the active semantic chain provides bidirectional narratives—both to articulate what stakeholders know explicitly and to trace back to the rationale for what they know implicitly (experience-related knowledge or common sense that are tacit, or background, knowledge).

The active semantic chain is distinctly different from the relationship among artifacts found in practice. In practice, requirements, analysis, design, implementation, and operations are physically and conceptually separate activities (discussed in detail in [58].

The active semantic chain is at the core of the Meta-Artifact's ability to promote understanding of the system. A key aspect of this understanding is documentation that is always current, temporally and spatially accessible, and represented from the stakeholders' viewpoint. Such documentation has been the dream and the nightmare of systems development since the first question about how a system worked. Because the integrated tools provide views tailored to the interests of stakeholders and based on all of the artifacts from which the current running system is derived, the documentation is far more comprehensive and timely than what is available in current practice.

The importance of this semantic chain and its many uses are well known, beginning with its foundations in the philosophy of science. Philosophers of science have written about the importance of capturing the genesis of ideas and the semantic chain of the artifacts that trace a development, whether a mathematical proof or a cultural tradition, from inception through to fruition. For example, William Dilthey [24] concludes:

> The study of the concepts and precepts of existing cultural systems suffers from their not having the process that led to them "... preserved in its original fluid form" but rather "objectified and compressed in the smallest possible form," i.e., in the shape of legal concepts.

Or as mathematician Henri Poincare observed in [62], we need to see "...the genesis [often a flash of intuitive insight] of our conceptions, in the proper sequence."

Adaptability: support for change within the current domain, e.g., for new target systems, changes to existing target systems, or technology insertion.

Background: a term used in Patriotta's knowledge management framework to refer to the tacit, unstated, and taken-for-granted assumptions underlying both individual and social practices [61]. With the passage of time, tacit knowledge from different periods forms layers in the background, with less likelihood that stakeholders will recall the explicit knowledge behind the tacit routines, or that a narrative will exist from which to recover the explicit knowledge (see information, explicit knowledge, narratives, and time).

Bifurcated Architecture (†): an architecture that separates the volatile variability, normally embedded in code, into an external database so that authorized users can directly change it. Volatile variability, also referred to as Business Rules, can be maintained more efficiently and accurately in an external database than when it is embedded in code and is more accessible for such purposes as analysis, audit, and training. The Bifurcated Architecture element of the Meta-Artifact Process (MAP) is orthogonal to the architecture-centric element of MAP because it is applied to the architecture derived through MAP, rather than driving the architecture development. This orthogonality preserves the architecture centricity of MAP based on all requirements, in contrast to other approaches to handling rules, e.g., rule-based or rules-centric approaches that drive the architecture development.

Bifurcated Architecture extends the domain analysis concepts of commonality and variability in two ways:

- Differentiating stable variability from volatile variability
- Providing physical as well as logical separation

Breakdowns: one of three lenses, along with time and narratives, used by knowledge management, a phenomenological approach to the study of knowing in the context of organizing. The three lenses provide operational devices to reveal the tacit, unstated, and taken-for-granted assumptions (referred to in *MSW* collectively as tacit requirements) underlying organizational practices by which organizational knowledge (a form of passive knowledge) is used by the organization's stakeholders on a day-to-day basis. Explicit knowledge that is in the foreground, e.g., when a system is under development (the social phenomenon of the development of the system is conspicuous as it is witnessed for the first time under the special circumstances of the system's conceptualization, design, and implementation), becomes part of the background (used by habit—the knowledge is deeply internalized and institutionalized so that it is used in an almost automatic and irreflexive way—or unused) after the system is in operation and performs tasks for stakeholders so that the stakeholders' knowledge of how the system performs those tasks is no longer conspicuous [61] (see knowledge management).

Breakdowns disrupt the system's routine operation (discontinuity in action), forcing stakeholders to again recall how the system performs its tasks. Along with the traditional view of a system breakdown as a failure to perform correctly, breakdowns provide a lens to focus on what would otherwise be tacit knowledge [61,65], e.g., embedded in the system and taken for granted. This focus discloses intentionality (why) and highlights the cognitive dimension (empirical how) of knowledge embedded in the system [65]. The Meta-Artifact, as a narrative articulated as artifacts (text, diagrams, etc.) of the knowledge creating dynamics of the system's development (see narratives), through the Active Semantic Chain, provides a means to convert information back to the knowledge needed to repair breakdowns (see time).

Business Rules: rules that represent the volatile variability of the application because they change in response to such things as the current situation—e.g., environmental conditions, technology, knowledge, and attitudes. Unlike domain rules, a system's business rules are under the control of the organization that uses the system. They capture the organization's business philosophy and practices in terms "… that describe, constrain, and control the structure, operations, and strategy" of the organization [39].

Business rules may be viewed as a constraint on particular applications in a domain. They may also be viewed as the decision-making rules for the application, within the invariants of the domain (represented by the domain rules). They are the same rules needed by decision support tools.

Business rules may be derived from external sources that the organization does not control, such as domain rules, regulations, and cultural considerations. This type of business rule reflects the organization's interpretation of how to comply with such external sources. The organization's interpretation may change in terms of both how to comply and which external sources are relevant. To the extent that the external source is itself subject to change (e.g., frequently revised federal regulations), the volatility is increased. Business rules may change very frequently (e.g., hourly or daily for online sales) or only a few times over the life of a system. In contrast, domain rules are unlikely to change over the entire life of the system. Regardless of the exact frequency, when business rules do change, externalizing them avoids costly maintenance activities.

Command and control: the exercise of authority and direction by a properly designated commander over assigned and attached forces in the accomplishment of the mission. Command and control functions are performed through an arrangement of personnel, equipment, communications, facilities, and procedures employed by a commander in planning, directing, coordinating, and controlling forces and operations in the accomplishment of the mission [21].

Commonality: similar functions and attributes across a group of applications. In OOT, these similarities are captured in derived classes through inheritance from base classes and through aggregation. Contrast with variability and see Domain Rules.

Control: verifying whether everything occurs in conformity with the plan adopted, the instructions issued, and the principles established, and then taking the appropriated corrective actions [28]. Many of the control needs of a system are captured in business rules.

Controls (†): by their nature, controls must test facts to determine if prescribed results have been met. That is, controls must enforce the constraints of the system. The controls considered here are the prescriptive rules implementing the business rules.

   During analysis and design, business rules would be identified for each active class. They would be converted during implementation to production rules to be executed by an inference engine (or other more tailored means), rather than program code. The production rules would be the mechanism for implementing the prescriptive instructions of the controls that enforce the business rules; they would be maintained in external files assigned to the components whose business rules they would enforce. The separation of the rules for each component would support a fundamental control procedure, separation of duties. Users authorized to maintain rules in one database could be physically prevented from changing rules in another database. Cohesion and separation can be further improved within the same database by using multiple packages for rules.

Control background: that part of the background in which tacit control needs are embedded, including systems that intentionally embed explicit knowledge for the purpose of carrying out tasks otherwise performed by people, accelerating the conversion of explicit knowledge to tacit knowledge by adding to the conversion caused by routinization of human tasks [61].

Domain Rules (†): the invariant rules that apply to systems in a domain, based on the underlying principles, theory, or traditions of the domain. Examples are doctrine in the military, information theory for engineering, and duality (debits and credits) for accounting. All applications (systems) for the domain must take account of the domain rules to determine which apply. Not all domain rules apply to every application of a domain, but each application must incorporate at least one of the domain rules in order to belong to the domain. The differences in domain rules applicable to one system, in contrast to another, reveal one possible partitioning of the domain.

Domain rules form the overarching category of requirements that characterize a domain by distinguishing it (and the systems that meet the needs for the domain) from other domains. Domain rules serve as meta-rules that govern what subordinate categories of requirements are appropriate for the domain. In this way, domain rules are constraints. They set the boundaries of a domain in pure problem space terms, by helping to identify requirements that lie inside the domain and that must be captured in systems for the domain.

On the one hand, domain rules are constraints. Domain rules help set the boundaries of a domain in pure problem space terms. On the other hand, they are part of the commonality (see commonality) of the domain. The commonality drives reuse, especially with OOT, where commonality can be incorporated through inheritance.

Domain Rules Analysis (†): an analysis that uses domain rules to help set the boundaries of the domain and, in conjunction with the volatile variability captured for the bifurcated architecture, to keep the focus on the problem domain until a comprehensive analysis is completed.

Explicit knowledge: active knowledge, embedded in the human consciousness, in contrast to passive knowledge that is written down, printed on paper, or stored on electronic devices and referred to as information [57,79] (see also knowledge management).

Extensibility: a capability for domain evolution, e.g., through accretion of other domains, environmental change, boundary expansion through new technology, or mandated boundary expansion through social, economic, or political change. This evolution by definition would be monotonic, in that the new aspects of the domain did not exist when the original domain was analyzed and would necessarily involve new concepts [33].

Foreground: explicit knowledge in contrast with background, which refers to implicit or tacit knowledge that is experience related, applied unconsciously, or taken for granted [61] (see knowledge management).

Framework: the set of class hierarchies for the domain and classes aggregated with classes in the hierarchy. Customary definitions using object orientation include patterns as part of the framework, but to reduce ambiguity, *MSW* [and 58] considers frameworks and patterns separately. The generalization–specialization relationship of hierarchies establishes the commonality (superclass) and variability (subclass or class from another hierarchy) among classes, which is a focus of OODA. Aggregated classes are included because, like generalization–specialization, aggregation only elaborates the definition of a class, unlike associations or the various dependency relationships that are used for patterns.

Information: passive knowledge, written down, printed on paper, or stored on electronic devices, in contrast to the active knowledge embedded in human consciousness [57] (see also knowledge management).

Integrated modeling tools: The UML is a commonly used modeling language that many vendors support with a wide range of modeling tools for MDD. These commercial-off-the-shelf (COTS) products include or are easily integrated with other COTS tools, such as code generation, requirements management, database management, continuous integration and delivery or deployment, and configuration management. IBM, for example, provides a range of integrated modeling tools for MDD, including IBM Rational Rose RealTime[1] (RRT) [38]. RRT, with the various COTS tools listed in this section, was used to make a complete prototype demonstrating all properties, qualities, and capabilities of MAP.

The modeling tools discussed here [e.g., 38] are tightly integrated, eliminating the need for duplicate efforts, so that the necessary artifacts for development—including documentation—are automatically produced as byproducts (see Figure 3.4 and the Special-Purpose Views section). The configuration management tool, for example, leverages the inherent support of UML-based RRT (e.g., packages of artifacts that can be worked on independently) for geographically and temporally dispersed collaborative development. The executable increments feed directly into continuous integration and delivery or deployment.

In fact, the core tool, RRT, performs the basic functions of many of the integrated modeling tools, offering substantial flexibility in determining which tools are needed for a project, based on, for example, its size. The inherent capabilities that the UML and OOT provide for collaborative development, such as packages and self-contained, encapsulated objects, are amplified through RRT's integrated publish-and-subscribe services. Iterative, incremental methods take full advantage of these capabilities and services.

A major advantage of a tool suite like that described in [38] is that code is generated from the visual model—for a large selection of target platforms. The tool is the central code and architecture manager, a key factor for enabling:

- Adaptability
- Extensibility
- Scalability

That is, the tool allows the insertion of external code from any source into architecturally correct locations, then manages it along with automatically generated code, reducing costs and preserving architectural integrity.

Figures G.1 and G.2 illustrate the role of integrated modeling tools in generating the active semantic chain of electronically linked artifacts. Figure G.1 shows how this semantic chain begins, using the familiar shape of a folder to represent a UML package, because the UML uses packages to collect whatever elements, including other packages, the developer chooses to organize the development project. The project organization itself has multiple views; e.g., the project manager may have a view oriented toward subsystem packages, whereas a developer of a subsystem may have views oriented toward packages for use-case realizations (references to use-case realizations or realization of use cases are based on the descriptions of such realizations in [9]), class structures, and behaviors. Arrows connecting packages show the relationships among packages, similar to cross-referencing among physical folders for hardcopy documents. These two figures also demonstrate one way the semantics are linked from high-level to lower-level details, by automatically propagating the names of the packages (see Figure G.1) and classes (see Figure G.2), for example.

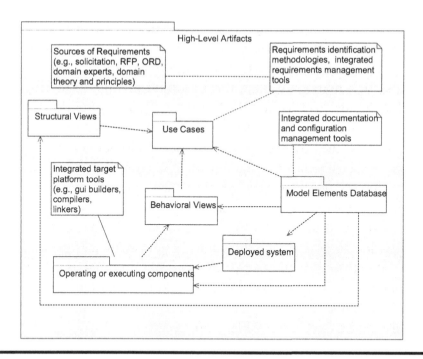

Figure G.1   Beginning of Active Semantic Chain.

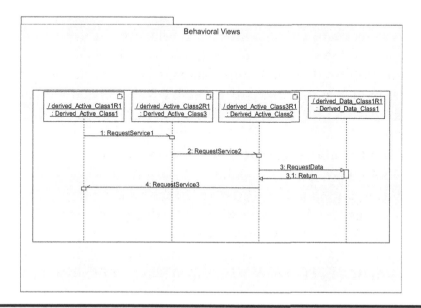

Figure G.2   Behavioral Link in Semantic Chain.

Ready access to the high-level semantics greatly assists developers in determining in subsequent iterations the detail that must be added and where, using the tools to capture the details, then managing them through their linkage to the high-level semantics to ensure they work together as intended.

The examples in Figures G.1 and G.2 are copies of the diagrams created by the tools from model elements in a database (see Figure 2.1, Database). The current state of the individual elements and the relationships among them are available for viewing and development activities, by applying the appropriate integrated modeling tools to the database. Any detail added to the elements would be automatically propagated into any existing or future diagrams containing that element—maintaining global consistency among the elements—greatly simplifying iterative development, management of collaborative development, and stakeholder participation.

Integrated modeling tools also support extensive structured and free-form annotations behind each diagram (such as the descriptions shown in the examples). In the model, detailed textual information may be entered for the icons and connecting lines. These details are readily accessible by simply double clicking on the item of interest. The elements of textual information reside in the same database as the visual elements of the model so that they are accessible to integrated modeling tools to extract for documentation or special-purpose views.

Knowledge Management: a phenomenological approach that looks at knowing through the three lenses of breakdowns, narratives, and time (see Glossary) in the context of organizing [61] (see also background, explicit knowledge, foreground, information, and tacit knowledge) (see Figure G.3).

Meta-Artifact (†): the electronically linked set of all of the artifacts of development, amplified by three extensions and five enabling technologies and its recursive use in MAP for its

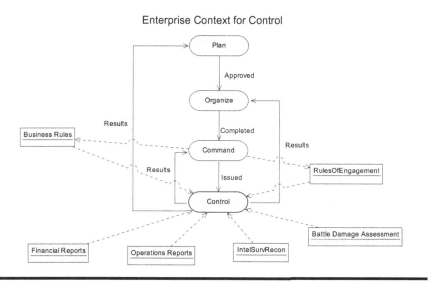

Figure G.3   Management Process.

own development. The Meta-Artifact provides a knowledge management narrative about a system that makes the background explicit. Narratives in knowledge management serve as a basic organizing principle of human cognition [61]. The Meta-Artifact continuously supplies the teleological remedy, through the active semantic chain, to the entropy that otherwise occurs with time, as development progresses and during operation and maintenance of the system, through its application in MAP, thereby converting knowledge captured in the Meta-Artifact into action and action into additional knowledge in the Meta-Artifact. The Meta-Artifact thus preserves the knowledge of the system and embedded in the system as explicit knowledge, preventing the knowledge from receding into history (becoming forgotten with the passage of time) and becoming tacit. By providing a means of identifying tacit knowledge contained in implicit domain rules, MAP helps convert previously tacit knowledge into explicit knowledge. The Meta-Artifact preserves the ontology of the problem and solution spaces.

The Meta-Artifact extends the modeling concept that the model is the application [52] by applying the concept to entire domains. The Meta-Artifact also extends the particulars of the concept beyond that of automatically generating code from the visual model (the basis for saying that the model is the application). That is, automatic code generation is just one of the subqualities noted for the Meta-Artifact.

More generally, the Meta-Artifact contrasts with the collection of artifacts produced in practice by methodologies other than MAP, including those produced for visual models from which code is generated, because of the interdependence the Meta-Artifact has with the other two extensions, Domain Rules Analysis, Bifurcated Architecture, and the five enablers. In particular, discussions of visual models in other methodologies do not refer to an active semantic chain with a central role in a development process designed to comprehensively analyze a complete domain (problem space) independently of the solution space, based on domain rules.

The Meta-Artifact provides the rules and structure for its own continued development. That is, the Meta-Artifact is used recursively in the incremental building of itself by MAP, analogous to the metacircular role of the UML metamodel [6], except that the UML metamodel is the starting point of the UML, whereas the Meta-Artifact is the goal of MAP. The Meta-Artifact goes beyond the role of metamodels and metadata, which provide the formalisms for defining other models or data, because it includes the completed artifacts themselves. MAP converts knowledge captured in the Meta-Artifact into action and action into additional knowledge in the Meta-Artifact.

Narratives: one of three lenses, along with time and breakdown**s,** used by knowledge management, a phenomenological approach to the study of knowing in the context of organizing. The three lenses provide operational devices to reveal the tacit, unstated, and taken-for-granted assumptions (referred to in *MSW* collectively as tacit requirements) underlying organizational practices by which organizational knowledge (passive knowledge) is used by the organization's stakeholders on a day-to-day basis.

> Narratives, articulated as texts, can be seen as material traces of learning and collective remembering processes, social imprints of a meaningful course of events, documents and records of human action. They allow people to articulate knowledge through discourse [61].

Stakeholders' knowledge of requirements is articulated through narratives and the narratives articulated as artifacts (the systems development equivalent of articulating narratives as text in knowledge management) for development and maintenance of the systems. For brevity these multiple steps for the transformation of requirements, whether explicit or tacit, into system artifacts (including code) are referred to collectively as articulating requirements (or knowledge) as artifacts.

When articulated as text (artifacts in the case of systems development), narratives allow the tracing of the process of articulating stakeholders' knowledge, including experience-related (tacit) knowledge, into the system through development artifacts. The narrative brings out the experience-related knowledge as part of the discourse conducted among stakeholders by articulating it along with other knowledge elicited from them. If the experience-related knowledge is challenged, e.g., by other stakeholders, additional narratives can be used to reconstruct the rationale underlying the experience-related knowledge, revealing the explicit knowledge that had become habit (see breakdown) or whose original purpose had been forgotten as it receded to the background (see time). Breakdowns expose a background that is otherwise taken for granted, e.g., the function of a system that no longer performs a task or a manual control that is no longer timely, exposing the assumption that the control will handle the event soon enough to avoid unacceptable loss. The layers created over time as explicit knowledge recedes to history offer the potential to uncover explicit knowledge in an earlier layer that was the origin of what is now tacit. The narrative lens works in conjunction with the lenses of breakdowns and time in rediscovering explicit knowledge by reconstructing evidence exposed by breakdowns or contained in earlier layers, reversing the knowledge creating dynamics [61].

This two-way application of narratives—both to articulate what stakeholders know explicitly and to trace back to the rationale for what they know implicitly (experience-related knowledge or common sense that are tacit, or background, knowledge) suggests that retaining the narratives (articulating them as artifacts) used in developing systems is worthwhile. During development of the system, the artifacts of development must be accessible and understandable (the social phenomenon of the development of the system is conspicuous as it is witnessed for the first time under the special circumstances of the system's conceptualization, design, and implementation) to be useful [61]. However, narratives or portions of narratives may not have been retained (articulated as artifacts). That is, the narratives or portions of them may have consisted of entirely oral communications, possibly augmented with temporary text, graphics, and demonstrations. The artifacts that are articulated, which emerged from preceding narratives (or portions of them) that were not retained, become disconnected from their experience-related or explicit knowledge (discontinuity in knowledge), i.e., there are links missing in the semantic chain of understanding for the artifacts. To have a complete semantic chain of understanding, all of the narratives ultimately leading to artifacts must be retained and be accessible to all stakeholders during the full lifecycle of the system. That is, if a narrative (or a portion of it) is retained, but put aside (e.g., stored in a medium or location not accessible to stakeholders) once the artifact it leads to is complete, the semantic chain of understanding is broken, producing gaps in understanding. The Meta-Artifact provides such a complete semantic chain, accessible through its active semantic chain.

Needs: a set of instructions comprising everything the system must do. Requirements are those needs that have been explicitly identified. Needs not explicitly identified as requirements are tacit requirements. There are needs that must be met by the system in order for it to be adequate, even if such needs are not identified as requirements. Tacit requirements are embedded in tacit knowledge (see tacit knowledge). The contrast between needs and requirements is important because assuming all needs are contained in the explicit requirements provided by stakeholders and in documents available to developers, such as an external solicitation or internal request, may lead to breakdowns.

Pattern: a collaboration, as defined in [9].

Problem space: the requirements and related information that describe the problem or need to be solved by the system. It is the reality the system must deal with by processing specified data to produce specified results from the requirements.

Routines: organization as a clockwork, based on successful responses to problematic situations. Once a specific routine has been invented, the problem addressed by it simply stops being a (conscious) problem, so routines become carriers of tacit knowledge [61].

Rule-based process: a process that is represented entirely by rules, with the reasoning strategy as well as the rule sets underlying the reasoning made explicit [36].

Rule-constrained process: an existing business process, implemented in conventional software code, which needs to have certain constraints enforced. These constraints may be externalized as rules [36].

Scalability: relative cost, time, and risk entailed for an application to process increased volumes beyond the capacity of the current platform configuration.

Solution space: the system or systems that meet the requirements in the problem space defined by the domain. The reality produced by the running system, which should match the reality of the requirements.

Stable variability (†): some variability, such as cycles in the AIS domain, would be stable because it would be based on the domain rules and other stable aspects of the domain such as traditional functions and processes. In OOT, stable variability would be captured through specialization during design in creating the framework (see framework), selecting from among the specialized classes in the framework during composition [33,35], and activation of services at runtime. The classes in the framework, including the derived classes specialized to capture the variability for different applications within the domain, as well as the related program code, would be stable. That is, the variability that distinguishes one application from another is not the source of volatility.

For example, the component to match depreciation expense with sales for a period would not be the same as the component to match direct materials costs with sales, but the portions of each component related to ensuring that appropriate components were invoked to match sales and expense for the accounting period (i.e., the domain rule for *Matching*) would be inherited. Furthermore, the specialized aspects of the two would seldom require change. There are basic depreciation methods that seldom change. What changes is which method to apply to a class of assets, which depends on the business rules.

Stakeholder: people who have a stake in the system, e.g., various developer disciplines, end-users, domain experts, managers, regulators, auditors, and certifiers [41].

Stakeholder view: how a stakeholder looks at the system [41], in terms of what it actually does or should do.

Tacit knowledge: implicit knowledge (referred to in *MSW* as a tacit requirement) that is experience-related, applied unconsciously, or taken for granted (see background and foreground) and embedded in human routines, organizational culture, and existing systems [61 and 65].

Time: one of three lenses, along with breakdowns and narratives, used by Knowledge Management, a phenomenological approach to the study of knowing in the context of organizing (see also information, explicit knowledge, and tacit knowledge). The three lenses provide operational devices to reveal the tacit, unstated, and taken-for-granted assumptions (referred to in *MSW* collectively as tacit requirements) underlying organizational practices by which organizational knowledge is used by the organization's stakeholders on a day-to-day basis. Knowledge, explicit at one time, e.g., when a system is under development (the social phenomenon of the development of the system is conspicuous as it is witnessed for the first time under the special circumstances of the system's conceptualization, design, and implementation), recedes to the background (becomes history and forgotten with the passage of time) at a later time, when the system is in operation and the knowledge used by stakeholders to make the system is no longer conspicuous.

Time provides a lens to understand the dynamics of stakeholder interaction (social becoming) underlying the process of knowledge construction in systems development organizations, i.e., viewing systems development as a social process to convert knowledge into a system. Time also provides a lens to see how knowledge entropically becomes information (discontinuity in time [61]. The information may be immediately useful, e.g., system documentation, or require extensive transformation to be useful, e.g. only the external behavior of the system as it is observed or inferred from previous outputs of the system. The combination of understanding the original teleological conversion of knowledge into the system (articulating requirements as artifacts) and the entropic conversion of that knowledge into information provides insight into countering the entropic conversion with the Meta-Artifact process, reverse engineering information to construct a Meta-Artifact after a system is made, and to use the Meta-Artifact to repair a system breakdown [61].

Variability: different functions and attributes across a group of applications. In OOT, these differences are captured in derived classes through specialization achieved by overriding or adding to functions and attributes inherited from base classes, by adding new base classes, and through aggregation (contrast with commonality). Some variability may be stable (see stable variability), but some may be volatile (see volatile variability). In the bifurcated architecture, volatile variability is allocated to an external repository.

View: see explicit definition in the Visual Representation of the Meta-Artifact section. Also see stakeholder view definition. In some literature, view is contrasted with viewpoint, but see [20].

Visible: something stakeholders of a system can actually see, such as the output of an automated system or the documents used in a manual system; also, the representations of an automated system that the stakeholders can see, especially a graphical representation or visual model.

Volatile Variability (†): represented by business rules, volatile variability is in contrast to the stability and commonality of domain rules and stable variability. The concept of volatile variability supplements the customary definitions of business rules by placing them in the context of commonality and variability and aiding in their identification during all phases of the system's lifecycle. That is, developers and stakeholders can apply the criterion of volatility—frequency of change—to identify functions to be externalized. The volatility criterion should make it unnecessary to have detailed definitions and rules for identifying business rules. While ultimately a matter of judgment as to whether the variability was volatile, the likely frequency of change would provide an objective measure. The frequency might vary from hourly to a few times over the lifecycle of the system, but regardless of the exact frequency, when business rules do change, allocating them to an external repository avoids costly maintenance activity.

Note

1 Migration to IBM Rational Software Architect RealTime Edition (RSARTE) is recommended as recently as April of 2022, but RRT was still supported as of March, 2021.

Bibliography

1   Adelman, Leonard. *Evaluating Decision Support and Expert Systems*. New York: Wiley, 1992.
2   Ambler, Scott. *The Object Primer*. 3rd ed. Cambridge: Cambridge University Press, 2004.
3   Arango, Guillermo, and Ruben Prieto-Diaz. "Introduction and Overview." *Domain Analysis and Software Systems Modeling*. Eds. Ruben Prieto-Diaz and Guillermo Arango. Los Alamitos, CA: IEEE Computer Society Press, 1991.
4   Beltratti, Andrea, Sergio Margarita, and Pietro Terna. *Neural Networks for Economic and Financial Modeling*. London: International Thomson Computer Press, 1996.
5   Ben-Ari, Mordecai. "Non-Myths about Computer Programming." *Communications of the ACM* 54.7 (2011): 35–37.
6   Bohner, Shawn Anthony. "A Graph Traceability Approach for Software Change Impact Analysis." Diss. George Mason University, 1995.
7   Booch, Grady, James Rumbaugh, and Ivar Jacobson. *The Unified Modeling Language Reference Manual*. Reading, MA: Addison-Wesley, 1999.
8   Booch, Grady, James Rumbaugh, and Ivar Jacobson. *The Unified Modeling Language Users Guide*. Reading, MA: Addison-Wesley, 1999.

9 Booch, Grady, James Rumbaugh, and Ivar Jacobson. *The Unified Software Development Process*. Reading, MA: Addison-Wesley, 1999.

10 Bruns, William J., Jr. *Accounting for Managers*. Cincinnati, OH: South-Western Publishing, 1994.

11 Cantor, Murray Cantor. "Rational Unified Process for Systems Engineering: Part 1: Introducing RUP SE Version 2.0." *The Rational Edge*, August 2003.

12 Case, Albert F., Jr. *Information Systems Development: Principles of Computer-Aided Software Engineering*. Englewood Cliffs, NJ: Prentice-Hall, 1986.

13 Coad, Peter, and Edward Yourdan. *Object-Oriented Analysis*. 2nd ed. Englewood Cliffs, NJ: Yourdan Press, 1991.

14 Coad, Peter, and Edward Yourdan. *Object-Oriented Design*. Englewood Cliffs, NJ: Yourdan Press, 1991.

15 Cohen, Sholom, and Linda M. Northrop. "Object-Oriented Technology and Domain Analysis." *IEEE Xplore*, 1998. DOI:10.1109/ICSR.1998.685733

16 Computer Science and Telecommunications Board, National Research Council. *Realizing the Potential of C4I, Fundamental Challenges*. Washington, DC: National Academy Press, 1999.

17 Davis, Alan M. *Software Requirements*. Revision. Upper Saddle River, NJ: Prentice Hall, 1993.

18 De Lucia, Andrea, et al. "Recovering Traceability Links in Software Artifact Management Systems using Information Retrieval Methods." *ACM Transactions on Software Engineering and Technology*, 16.4 (2007): Article 13.

19 DeMarco, Tom. *Structured Analysis and System Specification*. Englewood Cliffs, NJ: Yourdan Press, 1979.

20 Department of Defense. DoDAF Architecture Working Group. DoD Architecture Framework Version 2.02. May 2022.

21 Department of Defense. *Joint Technical Architecture, Joint Interoperability and Warrior Support Version 5*.0. April, 2003.

22 Desouza, Kevin C. "Managing Software Engineering Knowledge". *Knowledge Management Research & Practice* 2 (2004): 63–64.

23 Di Nitto, Elisabetta, and Alfonso Fuggetta. "Product Lines: What Are the Issues?" *IEEE* (1997).

24 Dilthey, William. *Survey of the System of the Particular Human Sciences, in which the Necessity of a Foundational Science Is Demonstrated*. Trans. Michael Neville. Braunschweig, Germany: Vieweg, 1896.

25 Dodig-Crnkovic, *Scientific Methods in Computer Science*. Vasterdas, Seeden: Department of Computer Science, Malardalen University. gordana.dodig-crnkovic@mdh.se

26 edX | Free Online Courses by Harvard, MIT, & more | edX. January 3, 2022. www.edx.org

27 Ehnebuske, Dave, *et al*. "Business Objects and Business Rules." *Business Object Workshop III, OOPSLA*. 1997.

28 Fayol, Henri. *General and Industrial Management*. 1916. Ed. Irwin Gray. Belmont, CA: David S. Lake Publishers, 1987.

29 Fraser, Steven, *et al*. "Application of Domain Analysis to Object-Oriented Systems." ***Addendum to the Proceedings OOPSLA '95*** (1995): 46–49.

30 Gamma, Erich, *et al*. *Design Patterns: Elements of Reusable Object-Oriented Software*. Reading, MA: Addison-Wesley, 1995.

31 Geers, Guido L. and William McCarthy. "Automated Integration of Enterprise Accounting Models Throughout the Systems Development Life Cycle." *Intelligent Systems in Accounting* 5 (1996): 113–128.

32 Gelinas, Ulric J. and Alan E. Oram. *Accounting Information Systems*. 3rd ed. Cincinnati, OH: South-Western College Publishing, 1996.

33 Gomaa, Hassan, *et al.* "A Knowledge-Based Software Engineering Environment for Reusable Software Requirements and Architectures." *INFT 803: Reusable Software Architectures: Course Readings.* Comp. and ed. Hassan Gomaa. Fairfax, VA: George Mason University, 1999.

34 Gomaa, Hassan. "An Object-Oriented Domain Analysis and Modeling Method for Software Reuse." *INFT 803: Reusable Software Architectures: Course Readings.* Comp. and ed. Hassan Gomaa. Fairfax, VA: George Mason University, 1999

35 Gomaa, Hassan. "Example of Domain Modeling Factory Automation Domain." *INFT 803: Course Notes on Object-Oriented Analysis and Modeling for Families of Systems.* Comp. and ed. Hassan Gomaa. Fairfax, VA: George Mason University, 1999.

36 Gottesdiener, Ellen. "Turning Rules into Requirements." *Application Development Trends* (July 1999).

37 Hay, David, and Keri Anderson Healy. *Guide Business Rules Project Final Report."* rev. 1.2. Chicago, IL: Guide International Corporation, 1997.

38 IBM Rational Software. "IBM Rational Rose RealTime: A Guide for Evaluation and Review." June 2003:1–19. April 2004. www-136.ibm.com/developerworks/rational/

39 ILOG. *Business Rules Powering Business and e-Business, White Paper.* Mountain View, CA: ILOG, 2001.

40 Imielinski, Tomasz, and Heikki Mannila. "A Database Perspective on Knowledge Discovery." *Communications of the ACM* 39.11 (1996): 58–64.

41 ISO/IEC JTC 1. "Systems and Software Engineering— Architecture Description." *ISO/IEC JTC 1 42010-2011* (2011). https://ieeexplore.ieee.org/servlet/opac?punum ber=6129465 (accessed on 6/11/2022).

42 Jacobson, Ivar, and Brian Kerr. *Use-Case 2.0: The Hub of Modern Software Development.* Ivar Jacobson International.

43 Joint Staff J3, Joint C4ISR Decision Support Center. *Joint Task Force (JTF) Command and Control (C2) Operational Concept Study, Phase 1 Final Report, 2001.*

44 Jones, Capers. *Applied Software Measurement.* 2nd ed. New York: McGraw-Hill, 1996.

45 Kang, Kyo C., *et al. Feature Oriented Domain Analysis (FODA) Feasibility Study.* Pittsburgh, PA: Carnegie Mellon University, 1990.

46 Ketz, J. Edward. *Bridge Accounting: Procedures, Systems and Controls.* Europe: Wiley, 2001.

47 Kruchten, Philippe. "Planning an Iterative Project." *The Rational Edge e-zine for the Rational Community.* October, 2002.

48 Kruchten, Philippe. *The Rational Unified Process.* Reading, MA: Addison-Wesley, 1999.

49 Kruse, Mark J. "Computers and Auditing." *Internal Auditor*, February, 1997,16–20.

50 Larsen, Robert. "A Continuous Early Validation Method for Improving the Development Process." Diss. George Mason University, 2000.

51 Levis, Alexander H., and Lee W. Wagenhals. *C4ISR Architecture Framework Implementation.* Fairfax: AFCEA Educational Foundation, 1999.

52 Lyons, Andrew. "UML for Real-Time Overview," *Rational Software Inc.* 1998.

53 McCarthy, William E. "The REA Accounting Model: A Generalized Framework for Accounting Systems in a Shared Data Environment." *The Accounting Review*, LVII.3 (1982): 554–578.

54 Metamodel.com. "What Is Metamodeling?" October 2003, 1–4. October 2003. www.metamodel.com/staticpages/index.php?page=20021010231056977

55 Meyer, Bertrand. *Object-Oriented Software Construction.* 2nd ed. Santa Barbara, CA: ISE Inc., 1997.

56 Morandin, Elisabetta, Gianfranco Stellucci, and Francesco Baruchelli. "A Reuse-Based Software Process Based on Domain Analysis and OO Framework." *IEEE* (1998): 890–891.

57 Mu¨ller-Merbach, Heiner. "Socrates' Warning Knowledge Is more than Information." *Knowledge Management Research & Practice* 2 (2004): 61–62.

58 O'Brien, Wayne. "Breakdowns in Controls in Automated Systems." Diss. George Mason University. 2008. Saarbrucken, Germany: Aktiengesellschaft & Co.

59 O'Brien, Wayne. "Avoiding Semantic and Temporal Gaps in Developing Software Intensive Systems." *Journal of Systems and Software* 81 (2008): 1997–2013.

60 OMG.org. April 2004. Object Management Group. April 2004. www.OMG.org

61 Patriotta, Gerardo. "On Studying Organizational Knowledge." *Knowledge Management Research & Practice* 2 (2004): 3–12.

62 Poincare, Henri. *Science and Hypothesis*. Trans. Francis Maitland. New York: Dover, 1952.

63 Polanyi, Michael. *Personal Knowledge Toward a Post-Critical Philosophy*. Chicago: The University of Chicago Press, 1974.

64 Polanyi, Michael. *The Study of Man*. Chicago: University of Chicago Press.

65 Polanyi, Michael. *The Tacit Dimension*. Garden City, NY: Doubleday, 1966.

66 Powers, Michael J., Paul H. Cheney, and Galen Crow. *Structured Systems Development*. 2nd ed. Boston, MA: Boyd & Fraser, 1990.

67 Pressman, Roger S. *Software Engineering: A Practitioner's Approach*. 4th ed. New York: McGraw-Hill, 1997.

68 Pressman, Roger S. *Software Engineering: A Practitioner's Approach*. 6th ed. New York: McGraw-Hill, 2005.

69 Rule Machines Corporation. *Managing Business Rules: A Repository Approach.* 1999.

70 Schlimmer, Jeffrey C., and Leonard A. Hermens. "Software Agents: Completing Patterns and Constructing User Interfaces." *Journal of Artificial Intelligence Research*, 1 (1993): 61–89.

71 Shaw, M., and D. Garlan. *Software Architecture: Perspectives on an Emerging Discipline.* Albuquerque, NM: Pearson, 1996.

72 Stedman, Craig. "Warehouse Managers Squeezed by User Demand, Limited Systems." *Computerworld* February 3, 1997, 45–46.

73 Stedman, Craig. "Warehouse Monitors in Demand." *Computerworld* February 17, 1997, 43–45.

74 Svoboda, Frank, *et al.* "Domain Analysis in the DoD." *ACM SIGSOFT Software Engineering Notes,* 21.1(1996): 57.

75 Swanson, G. A., and Hugh L. Marsh. *Internal Auditing Theory: A systems View.* New York: Quorum Books, 1991.

76 Tellis, Winston. "Application of a Case Study Methodology." *The Qualitative Report* 3.3 (1997): 1–17.

77 Weiss, Gerhard, ed. *Multiagent Systems.* Cambridge: MIT, 1999.

78 Wickens, Christopher D. *Engineering Psychology and Human Performance.* New York: HarperCollins, 1992.

79 Zave, Pamela. "Formal Methods Are Research, Not Development." *IEEE Computer* 29.4 (1996): 26–27.

Index

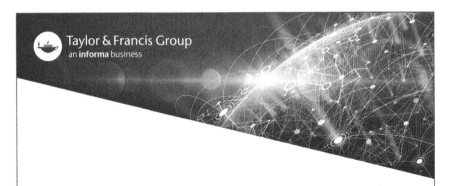

Printed in the United States
by Baker & Taylor Publisher Services